There is no person on planet I
death. It is not a question of 'if
the big picture questions that c
loss. Thankfully, Gabe Fluhrer l
resource that is engaging, clear
personally dealing with sufferil
someone who is, Fluhrer will he   ... right questions
and then point you to biblical answers.

Guy Prentiss Waters
Professor of New Testament, Reformed Theological Seminary,
Jackson, Mississippi

Experiencing pain and suffering is something Jesus and the apostles
warned us about if we are to grow as Christians. So we should not
be surprised when the fiery trial comes. But we often are. And
where to go for help? There are countless numbers of books, many
of them excellent, that deal with this topic, but Gabe Fluhrer's,
Why Do I Personally Experience Evil and Suffering?, will be the one
I will recommend from now on. True, he is a friend and a former
colleague, so you might expect me to say that. But I mean it. Dr
Fluhrer has one of the sharpest minds I have encountered, but in
this book he is sitting next to you as a friend and counsellor. You can
hear him speak too as he takes to the Scriptures and the gospel that
brings hope and joy amidst pain and suffering. A triumph.

Derek W. H. Thomas
Former Senior Minister, First Presbyterian Church, Columbia
South Carolina; Teaching Fellow, Ligonier Ministries

THE BIG TEN
Critical Questions Answered

SERIES EDITORS
James N. Anderson and Greg Welty

Why Do I Personally Experience Evil and Suffering?

Gabriel N. E. Fluhrer

CHRISTIAN
FOCUS

Copyright © Gabriel N. E. Fluhrer 2025

Paperback ISBN 978-1-5271-1299-5

E-book ISBN 978-1-5271-1388-6

10 9 8 7 6 5 4 3 2 1

Published in 2025
by
Christian Focus Publications Ltd,
Geanies House, Fearn, Ross-shire,
IV20 1TW, Great Britain.

www.christianfocus.com

Cover design by Daniel Van Straaten

Printed by Bell and Bain, Glasgow

CONTENTS

Dedication

To Chris Zaugg, brother, friend, and
follower of Jesus,
whose joyful faith in his Savior while
suffering has strengthened the
faith of many.

Acknowledgements

First and foremost, I am deeply grateful for the wise, patient, and meticulous editorial work of Drs. James Anderson and Greg Welty. To the extent that any reader is helped by this book, it is due to the insights and suggestions they offered throughout the process! Any remaining faults belong only to me.

I am also very thankful to the congregation, staff, and officers of the church I have the privilege of serving, First Presbyterian Church of Chattanooga, Tennessee. Their support has been invaluable.

The following individuals deserve special mention for their assistance while I was working on this project, though many more, no doubt, should be mentioned: Richard and Scottie Cain, Randy and Joan Nabors, Jerry and Kittie Stauffer, Lee and Lisa Paris, JR and Aimee Murphy, Mitch and Deborah Everhart, Skip Pond, Jane

Brown, Bruce Zeiser, Sara Kaitlin Van Puffelen, and Tommy and Jeanne Austin.

Finally, I thank God for my dear wife and children, who have borne the trials of life and ministry with me for almost two decades, with love and without complaint. They are God's greatest earthly gift to me!

Introduction

Jimmy Buffett died while I was working on this book. For readers unfamiliar with Buffett, he was a songwriter, singer, entrepreneur, and cultural icon for the last four decades. His music seemed to defy categorization. But everyone agreed that Buffett's songs were about a lifestyle that celebrated escaping reality, usually to a tropical paradise. His fans, known as 'Parrot Heads,' were cultish in their affection for the man. And they made him fabulously wealthy. At the end of his life, his net worth was north of $1 billion.

I grew up going to the coast of North Carolina for summer vacations. I can remember winding, sandy, two-lane byways, peppered with roadside stands selling fresh seafood. Jimmy Buffett was the soundtrack for these annual pilgrimages to the beach. His music was a part of my childhood and early adulthood for as long as I can remember.

Shortly after his death, I came across an article from a philosophy professor trying to make sense of the Buffett phenomenon. He put his finger on its essence. 'Half troubadour and half travel agent, Buffett has long been in the business of selling escape ... To love the music of Jimmy Buffett, in other words, is not to love life. It is to pessimistically admit that life is difficult and that it needs to be escaped every once in a while just to be endured.'[1] The author then made a comparison between Buffett's brand of escapism and the nineteenth-century philosopher Arthur Schopenhauer's argument that 'good art grows from a recognition of the difficulties of life, and it endeavors to respond to them by offering a momentary respite from its otherwise relentless slings and arrows.'[2] Having spent most of my academic life studying philosophy, I admit this comparison caught me off guard – in a good way (kudos to the author for bringing Germany and Key West, Buffet's unofficial headquarters, together!)

But I had some questions. For example, would the sophisticated Schopenhauer have recognized Buffett's

---

1. Drew M. Dalton, 'Jimmy Buffett, the "Parrot Heads" and the "Escape to Margaritaville:" A pessimistic 19th century outlook on hedonistic 20th century life,' https://fortune. com/2023/09/10/jimmy-buffett-parrot-heads-escape-to-margaritaville-philosophy/amp/, accessed September 13, 2023.

2. Ibid.

hit, 'Why Don't We Get Drunk,' as good art? I have my reservations.

All the same, I am certain that this professor was correct that Buffett built his empire on selling songs about escaping reality. I am also sympathetic to Schopenhauer's pessimism. We all know life is hard, and we welcome any relief we can find from its difficulties. So the analogy was fair.

What does that article have to do with what we'll study in this book? Both Buffett and Schopenhauer recognized that life is full of suffering, and both offered ways to cope with this difficult reality. This book tries to offer a different answer.

No one who reads what follows will think, 'I can't relate to that topic.' I don't say that out of an inflated sense of my abilities as a writer or because of an overheated ego! I say that because I think the title reveals maybe the most challenging question we will ever ask: 'Why do I personally experience evil and suffering?'

A previous book in this series explained (very well, in my opinion) a Christian answer to the *philosophical* problem of evil and suffering. In what follows, however, we will focus on the *personal* side of the problem.

Here is a good place to introduce a concept that will shape everything that follows: all of us are living out some kind of philosophy, whether we realize it or not.

So the personal and philosophical problems of suffering and evil always overlap.

But the personal problem of evil and suffering just feels, well, more *relevant*. Philosophical issues can seem theoretical, impractical, and speculative (although we'll see that this isn't the case). By contrast, suffering and evil hit us daily, wherever we are, whoever we are. Life's calamities are no respecter of persons.

For example, pick up your phone and open a news app. What do you read? Evil and suffering, with just enough of those annoying ads to take your mind off the horror of it all, even for a moment. Reflect on your past week. What did you experience? Evil and suffering, to some degree. Think about the conversations you've had in the last few days. Once again, I would wager that the people you spoke with experienced evil and suffering at some point, however small or large. None of our lives are left untouched by these awful realities.

Still, as I hinted at above, we all have a philosophy of life, so, at some level, we are already answering the question of personal suffering and evil. These answers are shaped by what we think the world is like, what we think is fair, what we expect out of life, and so on – all inescapably philosophical considerations. So, while philosophical concepts can appear irrelevant, they have massive practical implications.

Given the fact that we're trying to deal with personal suffering and evil from some philosophical position or another, let's ask another question: are our answers *working*? Are we finding peace and even joy in the midst of our trials? At this point, an irritated voice in our head demands, 'How can anyone find peace, let alone joy, when life is so hard?!'

If that's our response, then maybe our answers aren't working. Maybe you've tried methods, techniques, or read other books to alleviate the pain of life, all to no avail. I can't promise this book will change your life. But I can promise that the responses given here will be grounded in the Bible, which *can* change your life.

The Bible offers answers most people don't take the time to consider, so I would simply ask for your patience as you read. Keep an open mind to the Bible's point of view, because it has *a lot* to say about our afflictions. After all, it is a record of ordinary people, like you and me, who faced crushing circumstances and ended up praising God despite them. That sounds like a new, very attractive way to cope with life's difficulties!

Even so, we may find ourselves skeptical, even cynical, at the thought that the Bible could help us. Finding comfort in the midst of our trials and tragedies may seem like a hopeless fantasy – like that vacation you daydream about, but know will never happen. But the

Bible assures us that such comfort is not a fantasy. It is not out of our reach.

Besides, skepticism and cynicism are no way to go through life. The Scriptures offer us a better way, holding out the promise that we can make joy and peace our new normal, come what may.

I want to make that case in what follows. We'll start in chapter 1 with a brief overview of some basic biblical principles that can help us answer this question. In chapter 2, we'll look at some alternatives to the Christian perspective and see if they help us. From there, chapters 3–5 examine what the Bible says on certain issues, from depression to death to disabilities. Of course, we won't be able to cover every conceivable problem we might face. But we'll try to give attention to the ones that weigh so many of us down. Chapter 6 addresses some of the most frequently asked questions related to this question. Finally, chapter 7 concludes our study with a uniquely biblical presentation of how to live in a world beset by evil and suffering.

My goal, therefore, is simple and ambitious. I want us not just to *survive* when suffering and evil come our way. I want us to *thrive* amid them.

That's a lofty aspiration! But I don't think it's unreasonable. I've been a pastor for almost twenty years now and I can attest, both from my life and the lives of countless others, that God can give us joy, despite our circumstances. I've witnessed people live as I described, in real time. I'm constantly amazed by their faith, confidence, joy, and hope when tragedy strikes.

Responding with hope and joy are not just for the spiritual elite, however. You too can begin to live like this. All we must do is listen to God – the personal, powerful, caring heavenly Father of Scripture – speaking to us in His Word. That's what we'll try to do in this book – listen and learn from the One who made us, knows us, and cares deeply about our hurts and heartaches.

1

How Do We Begin to Answer This Question?

'Can you help me with this problem, Dad?' My teenage daughter looked up from her math homework. I thought to myself, 'Can I help you? Of course not! You're in a math class in 11th grade that I wasn't in when I started college!' But I kept my thoughts to myself and said, 'Sure, sweetie. Let's have a look.' I stared intently at the mystifying symbols before me, but I knew the moment I looked at the problem, I had no idea how to help her. She knew it too and wasn't buying my bluff. 'It's OK, Dad. I'll ask the teacher tomorrow,' she said, in that tone that, in the South means, 'Bless your heart, daddy. You're clueless.'

I'm hardly a candidate for 'Dad of the Year Award' in any category, let alone 'Math Homework Helper.' But we all feel a bit defeated when we can't help someone we love, *especially* when we want to help.

We feel the most helpless when someone who is suffering comes to us for answers. We so badly want to say the right thing, do the right thing, do anything to help. But the problems in our lives and the lives of our friends and loved ones seem so overwhelming we end up feeling like we do more harm than good in these situations.

Even more acute is the question of God's role in our suffering, if any. One book I was reading not too long ago gives poignant voice to our most important questions about God and suffering. 'What is God up to when He makes us wait and wait for His deliverance? Why would a loving, sovereign God leave us stuck in a situation of painful suffering, when He could so easily and swiftly solve all our problems for us?'[1] For many of us, these are *the* questions.

Throughout this book, I will argue the Bible can help us – and others – with our most unsettling questions in life. Before I make my case, however, we need to step back and look at some of our basic cultural 'givens,' so that we can begin to understand why the Bible's answers so often appear unpersuasive.

THREE ASSUMPTIONS TO UNDERSTAND – AND QUESTION
The sad reality of life is that all of us must answer the question this book asks. All of us do, in fact, answer it

---

1. Iain M. Duguid and Matthew P. Harmon, *Living in the Light of Inexhaustible Hope: The Gospel According to Joseph* (Phillipsburg, NJ: P&R Publishing, 2013), p. 62.

– every day. But what shapes our answer? As we talked about in the introduction, we all have a philosophy of life. So, we can identify certain assumptions that inform our response to suffering, developed by powerful forces that we don't often recognize. Let's look at a few of them.

The first is the idea that *you can't trust anyone*. We learn this lesson early. Maybe it was an absent parent, a father or mother who was supposed to be there for you, but wasn't. Maybe it was abuse at the hands of a loved one. Maybe it was the humiliating experience of being bullied or excluded. All of us can reach back into our memories and recall the first time we realized that when you trust other people, you will get hurt. Those moments of hurt and heartache, tiny or gargantuan, end up shaping us into the people we are. We carry them with us. We try to let go, but they are stubborn. They stick to us like that stain you can't get off your favorite shirt.

Many psychologists and therapists explain this problem in terms of attachment. One of the leading researchers on attachment theory explains, 'the quality of connection to loved ones and early emotional deprivation is key to the development of personality.'[2] Based on her research findings (and many others), I think she's on to

---

2. Dr. Sue Johnson, *Hold Me Tight: Seven Conversations for a Lifetime of Love* (New York: Hachette Book Group, 2008), p. 17.

something. For many of us, we tried to get close to others and we learned that they were not safe.

The second assumption is that *your destiny is up to you.* After being let down, let go, and left out, we begin to reason this way: 'I can't count on other people. So, life is up to me.' This answer seems very plausible in the modern West. We have so much at our fingertips that gives us the illusion of control. We can check the weather or buy a car with a few taps on our phones. We feel powerful. Grasping our smartphones, we feel the force of William Ernest Henley's words, 'I am the master of my fate, I am the captain of my soul.' Let's be honest: we feel like little gods.

But, once again, life shatters our illusion of control. We eat all the right foods and exercise, only to have the doctor close the door behind her with a concerned look on her face after reading our charts. We invest in a home security system with every upgrade offered and still the thief finds a way in. Don't mistake my point – we should plan, save, watch what we eat, take precautionary measures, etc. But, in the end, for every contingency we think we've covered, there is another one we didn't expect.

Hence our general feeling of anxiety in the Western world. We have the most material abundance of any generation in the history of mankind, yet we're also the most fretful. Think about that. What so much of the world has worried about for so long – where our next meal is coming from, where to find clean water, how to live past age thirty – hardly ever crosses our minds. With so much, why are we so uneasy?

Lots of answers could be given, but the point here is that, even though we don't have to worry about the basic necessities of life, we still feel a general sense of apprehension. In response, we try to calm our nerves with the promising anesthetic of control. But whatever mastery we imagine we have over our lives turns out to be like thinking a piece of paper will keep you safe in the middle of a hurricane. A woman who mentored my wife years ago summed up our predicament in a few words: 'Life never lets up.'

A third cultural assumption that seems like gospel truth is that whatever God or gods may exist they *are absent from your pain and struggle*. Not only is life up to us, the gods presented to us are impotent, we are told. All the world's religions grapple with the issue of suffering. Every philosopher worth his or her salt has pondered it. But they almost always come to the same conclusion: Suffering is a fact of life and we're on our own and God or the gods can't help us.

These cultural assumptions are powerful and subtle. But they are real. Of course, there are others we could name. But we need to acknowledge at least these three before we can be open to the Bible's answers on personal suffering and evil.

CAN OTHER RELIGIONS AND PHILOSOPHY HELP US?

At the risk of oversimplification, here's the way every world religion tries to answer this question (Christianity excepted). They offer us gods that are either too big or too small. Let me explain. On the one hand, we're told God (if he/she/it exists) is so transcendent – so far removed from the affairs of this world – that He[3] is not really involved in the day-to-day lives of His creatures. Such involvement would be beneath the deity. Now, you might fear such a god, but you will never trust Him or love Him. And you certainly won't think He can really help you when life gets hard. How could a god so far removed from earth have any sympathy for us puny sufferers?

On the other hand, prior generations were told that there were countless gods who were little more than exaggerated humans. They fought, ate, committed adultery, did superhuman feats, and so on. Again, like humans, just 'bigger.' But, supposing such beings exist, even they can't really help us. None of them are all-powerful. When the dust of suffering settles, they stare

---

3.   Since I am writing as a Christian, I will use the male pronoun 'He' when referring to God.

back at us and shrug, as if to say, 'Sorry, wish there was more I could do, but I can't.'

As a result, here's the conundrum the world's religions offer us: a disinterested god, or impotent gods, or some combination of both. You may think I'm being unfair in this analysis. But we'll examine these solutions in more detail in the next chapter.

If religion can't help us, maybe philosophy will save the day. After all, the word *philosophy* comes from two Greek words that mean 'love of wisdom.' If anything, we need wisdom when we suffer. There are myriad answers that various schools of philosophy have offered to the question of personal suffering and evil. We don't have the space to examine them all, so I want to focus on what is likely the most popular option today.

The dominant philosophy of our time is called *materialism* or *naturalism*. This is the view that only material entities exist. There are no gods, there is no soul, and there is no life after death. We'll see an example of this kind of thinking in chapter 3.

This view seems to raise more questions than it answers. For example, if we are the products of energy, matter, and chance, then, at root, the source of everything is impersonal. If this is what we presuppose about our most basic reality, the problem becomes explaining how things like love, justice, beauty – *personal* experiences –

arose in an ultimately impersonal universe. For, nothing matters if matter is all there is.

Naturalism seems plausible because it is supposedly based on scientific reasoning. 'Science has shown us that the material universe is all there is,' the argument goes. Of course, science has shown no such thing and it never can. Science is incapable of proving this claim. To be clear, I am not anti-science! Instead, I am trying to point out a few problems with this argument. First, naturalism in general and science in particular are ill-equipped to answer the question of personal suffering and evil. Second, naturalism's influence on science can and should be questioned, both philosophically and scientifically. If naturalism cannot make sense of love or justice or beauty, then we have good reason to think it cannot help answer the main question of this book.

Third, when the waves of suffering and evil come crashing over our lives – as they inevitably will – the prospect of a mindless, purposeless universe becomes somewhat less appealing, to put it mildly. Naturalism may seem to work on the sunny days, but when the storms of life come with gale force winds to our doorstep, we don't *act* like materialists or naturalists. We may affirm naturalism as a philosophy, but few of us *live* as if the universe is all there is. When disaster tears a hole in our daily routines, we find out what we really believe. At that moment, we all want to know there is a reason for the hurt and pain we experience. We want to know that life is not a cold, impersonal, meaningless joke. We crave that secure attachment mentioned above. As a Christian, I would say we are craving a secure attachment with God.

Even if you don't share my Christian faith, I think the overall argument I am presenting rings true. All of us suffer and, when we do, we have an insatiable desire to know why. If you've tried a certain philosophy or religion to help you and still find yourself searching, then I would ask you to keep reading. There is a better answer to the question of personal suffering and evil than those offered by world religions and various schools of philosophy.

A BETTER ANSWER

If the answers outlined above won't really help us, what will? You may be skeptical when I say this, but I think the Bible provides us with not just the best, but the *only* answer to the despairing question of our personal suffering and evil. I'll try to make my case as we go along, and I don't want to get ahead of myself. Before we can understand how the Bible helps us with our pain, we need to know what it is all about.

The Bible was written over roughly two millennia by about three dozen human authors. They had different cultural contexts, different life experiences, and different goals when they wrote. Yet, behind all the human authors is one Author, God Himself. The Bible tells us that God wrote it, ultimately. 'All Scripture is breathed out by God' (2 Tim. 3:16). [4] When I first became a Christian and began studying the Bible, one of the many things that astonished me was how so many people, from such varying times and places, wrote such a consistent message. The verse I just cited tells us why. God superintended history and the life situations of the various human authors to give us precisely the words and message He wanted us to have.

Is the Bible then just a collection of religious thoughts from particularly spiritual people who lived a long time ago? Not at all. It claims to be God's *living* Word for today, thousands of times. Not just any god's word, but *the* Word of *the* living God, the creator of heaven and earth. 'But,' you might ask, 'a lot of other books claim to be revelations of God. Why should we trust the Bible over those?'

A full answer is beyond the scope of this book, so I'll refer you to some resources. [5] For now, we will spend a

---

4. Bible references such as Genesis 1:1 refer to the book called Genesis, to the first chapter of that Bible book, and specifically to the first verse of that chapter. Thus 'bookname xx:yy' refers to chapter xx, verse yy of the book by that name. Most versions of the Bible have a table of contents with page numbers to help readers locate each book by name.

5. For a worthy defense of the Bible's reliability, see the volume in this series by Timothy Paul Johnson, *Why Should I Trust the Bible?* (Christian Focus, 2020). Two of the best books I've read

large part of this study discussing why we can trust the Bible's answers to our questions about evil and suffering, as opposed to those offered by other worldviews. Over the course of these pages, I hope you will begin to see that this is not empty rhetoric. Instead, I trust you will see for yourself that the Bible can answer our questions on these vexing issues precisely because it is *true*.

FIVE BEDROCK TRUTHS FOR OUR STUDY

To that end, five bedrock truths will shape the rest of what follows. These truths will change how we understand personal suffering and evil, if we are willing to accept them and believe them.

They will not make our pain go away. They are not like a magic pill we can take and everything will suddenly be fine. But if we taste them, imbibe them, and let them have their way with us, we will begin to find what proves so elusive – peace in the midst of trials.

BEDROCK TRUTH #1: GOD IS SOVEREIGN

We must start here. From the opening verse of the Bible, Genesis 1:1, to the last verse of the Bible, Revelation 22:21,

---

that demonstrate the Christian worldview's unique ability to make sense of reality are James N. Anderson, *Why Should I Believe Christianity?* (Christian Focus, 2016) and John M. Frame, *Apologetics: A Justification of Christian Belief*, 2nd Ed., ed. Joseph E. Torres (P&R Publishing, 2015).

God offers Himself to us as completely sovereign over everything in the universe, seen and unseen, all the time. Here is a sampling of verses that demonstrate this reality:

> The LORD kills and brings to life; he brings down to Sheol and raises up. The LORD makes poor and makes rich; he brings low and he exalts. (1 Sam. 2:6-7)

> Our God is in the heavens; he does all that he pleases. (Ps. 115:3)

> I form light and create darkness; I make well-being and create calamity; I am the LORD, who does all these things. (Isa. 45:7)

> Are not two sparrows sold for a penny? And not one of them will fall to the ground apart from your Father. (Matt. 10:29)

> For from him and through him and to him are all things. To him be glory forever. Amen. (Rom. 11:36)

> He upholds the universe by the word of his power. (Heb. 1:3)

> Worthy are you, our Lord and God, to receive glory and honor and power, for you created all things, and by your will they existed and were created. (Rev. 4:11)

Like I said, this is a tiny sampling of the Bible's teaching on the sovereignty of God. This understanding of God is out of fashion today, as it always has been. Why? Because one of the chief characteristics of being sinners is that we want to be little sovereigns. Our *pretended* sovereignty and God's *actual* sovereignty are on a collision course in every human heart, every day, in every age. This is *the* chief battle of our heart, which we can put in question form: 'Will we let God be God?'

We need to be careful here. God is sovereign. He rules over every creature. Nothing is outside His control. Whatever happens in our lives is part of His plan. This is the clear, indisputable teaching of the Bible.

To modern ears, that sounds authoritarian and dangerous. That's why I said we need to be careful. The picture the Bible paints in such luxuriant colors of God's sovereignty is not that of an angry despot or an abusive narcissist. Instead, the brushstrokes combine to offer us a painting of indescribable beauty and comfort.

You see, the Bible tells us that this sovereign God of the universe exercises His power *in love*. He is not power-hungry, but life-giving. He is not capricious, but caring. He is not dangerous, but delightful. He is not authoritarian, but affectionate. He does not apologize for being sovereign, but He also does not lord it over us like a dictator. His authority is gentle and His gentleness never undermines His authority.

The great early church theologian and philosopher Augustine takes us by the hand and stands us in front of this breathtaking painting of God's sovereignty with these words: 'You are the true, sovereign joy ... you who are sweeter than all pleasure, though not to flesh and blood, you who outshine all light and yet are hidden deeper than any secret in our hearts, you who surpass all honor, though not in the eyes of men who see all honor in themselves.'[6]

One final caveat. Though God is totally sovereign, that does not make us puppets on a string. We have free will, in a qualified sense. We'll unpack in what sense that is in the next chapter.

For now, if we don't grasp the sovereignty of God, or we refuse to believe it, we will never make sense of life, much less the hardships of life. We'll examine the implications of this first truth as we go along, but, again, we have to start here or nothing else will make sense.

BEDROCK TRUTH #2: SIN IS REAL

One of my classmates in a graduate course was a delightful, brilliant, thoughtful, and kind attorney,

---

6. St. Augustine, *Confessions*, X.1, trans. R.S. Pine-Coffin (New York: Penguin Books, 2015), p. 261.

who had just retired from practicing law. He was also Jewish, though not particularly devout. We struck up a friendship quickly and I soon found myself at one of the best Jewish delis in Philadelphia, about to enjoy a really good lunch.

He knew I was a pastor and was intrigued that I was studying philosophy. So, he asked me, 'You believe all the basic doctrines of Christianity, right?' I nodded, as I enjoyed every bite of the sandwich. 'What about original sin? Surely you don't believe in that?' I swallowed. 'Yes, I do,' I replied.

He got mad. Not at me but at the thought that someone who was apparently educated (he misjudged me on that one) would believe such a monstrous doctrine, as he called it.

My friend's reaction to the doctrine of original sin is standard fare today. Original sin is the teaching that we inherit a corrupt moral nature from Adam.[7] More precisely, because of Adam's sin, every one of our faculties is now corrupted. As with truth #1, this truth is horribly offensive to modern sensibilities, maybe even more so. In fact, it might be the most offensive teaching of orthodox Christianity.

---

7. Robert Letham, *Systematic Theology* (Wheaton, IL: Crossway, 2019), p. 381.

Why? Because we've been taught that all people are basically good.[8] This assumption informs every area of life today, from law, to politics, to science, to art. Question this secular doctrine and you might as well be on the same level as people who wear tin foil hats.

I find the vitriolic reaction to original sin puzzling. I can understand someone questioning God's sovereignty. But original sin should be easy to believe because we have so much evidence for it! Daily. Minute by minute. Not only all around us, but also within us. As the British writer and Christian apologist G. K. Chesterton put it, 'Certain new theologians dispute original sin, which is the only part of Christian theology which can really be proved.'[9]

The Bible does not mince words when teaching us this truth. Again, here is a sampling:

> The LORD saw that the wickedness of
> man was great in the earth, and that every
> intention of the thoughts of his heart was
> only evil continually. (Gen. 6:5)

---

8. For example, a recent study found that most Americans think they are morally superior to those around them. See Cindi May, 'Most People Consider Themselves Morally Superior' https://www.scientificamerican.com/article/most-people-consider-themselves-to-be-morally-superior/, accessed March 9, 2024.

9. G. K. Chesterton, *Orthodoxy* (Ignatius Press, 1995), p. 19.

Can the Ethiopian change his skin or the leopard his spots? Then also you can do good who are accustomed to do evil. (Jer. 13:23)

Behold, I was brought forth in iniquity, and in sin did my mother conceive me. (Ps. 51:5) NOTE: David is not saying the sexual act of procreation was sinful, but that he was sinful from birth.

None is righteous, no, not one; no one understands; no one seeks for God. (Rom. 3:10-11)

Therefore, just as sin came into the world through one man, and death through sin, and so death spread to all men because all sinned. (Rom. 5:12)

As you can see, the Bible teaches that we are sinful to the core of our being. As the old phrase has it, we are not sinful because we sin; we sin because we *are* sinful.

You might have heard the term 'total depravity.' Total depravity follows directly from original sin. It teaches that if all of us are tainted by Adam's fall, then every part of us is affected by sin. Our minds, emotions, intellect, will – every part of our inner life is inclined to sin. That's what we mean by total depravity.

We should distinguish *total* depravity from *utter* depravity. The two are not synonymous. Total depravity says every faculty of a human being is affected by sin. Utter depravity says that we are as bad as we could be. We are not as bad as we could be, because of what theologians call 'common grace' (Matt. 5:45), which simply means God enables us to be better than we would be if left to ourselves. Every part of us is affected by sin, but we are not as sinful as we could be. That is a tender mercy of the Lord.

Original sin resulting in total depravity is one of the chief reasons there is so much evil in the world and in our lives. If we miss this truth, we miss a key component of biblical teaching on personal evil and suffering.

BEDROCK TRUTH #3: SATAN IS ACTIVE

When we hear the name 'Satan,' the image of a guy with a pitchfork, horns, and a bad moustache comes to mind. The idea of a personal devil is preposterous to most people. But, again, the Scriptures make it clear that the devil is very real and very active.

> Now the serpent was more crafty than any other beast of the field that the LORD God had made (Gen. 3:1). As the verse from Revelation below will make clear, the serpent here refers to the devil.

> The LORD said to Satan, 'From where have you come?' Satan answered the LORD and said,

'From going to and fro on the earth, and from walking up and down on it.' (Job 1:7)

And [Jesus] was in the wilderness forty days, being tempted by Satan. (Mark 1:13)

'Simon, Simon, behold, Satan demanded to have you, that he might sift you like wheat.' (Luke 22:31)

And the great dragon was thrown down, that ancient serpent, who is called the devil and Satan, the deceiver of the whole world – he was thrown down to the earth, and his angels were thrown down with him. (Rev. 12:9)

According to the Bible, Satan is a personal, active, and powerful being. He is not a demi-god, however. He is not all-knowing or all-present, like God. He is still a creature, but he is an extremely powerful creature.

As with original sin, so with the existence of the devil: I do not find it that hard to believe that Satan is real because I see so much evidence of his activity. To be sure, I do not mean that Satan or his demons are the cause of all the suffering and evil we endure. But he is responsible for some of it. Therefore, we ignore the reality of Satan and his minions to our peril.

Even non-Christians recognize the reality of a personal devil. National Public Radio journalist Scott

Simon says he always avoided using the word 'evil' when covering terrible events around the globe. He was 'of a generation educated to believe that "evil" was a cartoonish moral concept.'

All of that changed when he and his daughters saw the images from a chemical weapons attack in Syria in 2017. These images affected him in a profound way. Here's how he describes what happened next:

> We watched in silence. I've covered a lot of wars, but could think of nothing to say to make any sense. Finally, one of our daughters asked, 'Why would anyone do that?' I still avoid saying 'evil' as a reporter. But as a parent, I've grown to feel it may be important to tell children about evil, as we struggle to explain cruel and incomprehensible behavior they may see not just in history … but in our own times … I've interviewed Romeo Dallaire, who commanded U.N. peacekeeping forces in Rwanda in 1993 and 1994 when more than 800,000 Tutsi Rwandans were then slaughtered over three months. Dallaire said that what happened made him believe in evil, and even a force he called the devil. 'I've negotiated with him,' he told us, 'shaken his hand. Yes. There is no doubt in my mind … and the expression of evil to me is through the devil and the devil at work and possessing human beings and turning them into machines of destruction. … And one of the evenings in my office, I was looking out the window and my senses felt that something was there with me that shifted me. I think that evil

and good are playing themselves out and God is monitoring and looking at how we respond to it.'[10]

The U.N. official Simon interviewed had no problem believing in the devil because he had a front row seat to such inexplicable cruelty. The best and only explanation was that a real, personal devil was active in the world we inhabit.

Bedrock Truth #4: The Savior Is Sweet

If God is absolutely sovereign, we are totally sinful, and the devil is actually real, then we need a Savior. The Bible tells us that Jesus is the only Savior for sinners. Therefore, He is sweet. This bedrock truth is indispensable when we go through suffering and evil. This is why I have chosen to describe Jesus and knowing Him as 'sweet.'

We must taste, as it were, the sweetness of Jesus. By this I mean that He must not be simply a concept, a good idea, or an object of admiration. We must know Him intimately, or suffering and hardship will break us. We must, with the psalmist of old, 'taste and see that the LORD is good!' (Ps. 34:8).

Jesus is sweet especially when we suffer because His whole life He suffered. He was born into and

---

10. Scott Simon, 'A Meditation on "Evil",' https://www.npr.org/2017/04/08/523058634/a-meditation-on-evil, accessed September 10, 2024.

lived in poverty. He was unjustly accused, tortured, mocked, abused, and then subjected to one of the most cruel forms of execution ever devised by sinful humans. Therefore, the prophet Isaiah foretold that Jesus would be 'a man of sorrows and acquainted with grief' (Isa. 53:3).

As we said above, the Bible makes it clear that Jesus was and is the incarnate God of the Old Testament. Stop and think about that. The Scriptures say that the God who made everything became a human. He was a baby, a toddler, a teenager, and a young adult. He worked with His hands. He learned to read, write, and count. He had siblings. He experienced normal life like countless people have throughout the ages.

How could the God who knows all things learn anything? How could the One who designed the cell become a human being dependent on cell development? These questions highlight the glorious mystery of the incarnation. Jesus was fully human and fully God. He could say, on the one hand, 'I thirst.' On the other hand, He could say, 'Before Abraham was, I am,' (John 8:58) – a direct claim to deity, since the God of the Old Testament identified Himself as the great I AM (Exod. 3:14). While these statements seem contradictory, they are not. Instead, they highlight the amazing difference between the biblical God and every other option.

That difference makes all the difference. Simply put, in the Bible, we meet the only God anywhere who can sympathize with us. As shame researcher and TED Talk sensation Brené Brown put it, 'The two most powerful words when we're in a struggle [are] "Me too".'[11] At once transcendent, yet like us in every way (except sin), Jesus is the only God in the history of the human race who can enter into our problems and suffering and say, 'Me too.'

The Son of God, the eternal second person of the Trinity,[12] takes a body and soul to Himself, is born in space-time history, and experiences all the infirmities and calamities of life in a fallen, sinful world. No one would make this story up.

In fact, Jesus' life story gets better for us as it gets worse for Him. As we follow Him through the pages of the New Testament, we see Him born into poverty and living a life of obscurity for some three decades before He begins His public ministry. The Son of God was what we would call a blue-collar worker. He had calloused hands,

---

11. Brené Brown, 'Listening to Shame,' TED Talk, 19:10, https://www.ted.com/talks/brene_brown_listening_to_shame?language=en, accessed January 11, 2024.

12. The Trinity refers to the biblical teaching that God is one God in three persons – Father, Son, and Holy Spirit. For further study, see Michael Reeves, *Delighting in the Trinity: An Introduction to the Christian Faith* (Downers Grove, IL: IVP Academic, 2012).

long days, aching muscles, and dirty clothes. He smelled bad. He never had a girlfriend, let alone a wife. He never had sex. He never went to college.

Not even His own family understood Him. His mother, who had a supernatural visitation from an angel about her Son's birth, seems to have questioned His ministry (Mark 3:21, 31). Misunderstood, overlooked, underpaid, underappreciated. Can you relate?

Then He began His public ministry. From the moment He started preaching, He faced determined opposition, from the religious authorities of His day, ironically. He hadn't gone to the right Rabbinical schools. He wasn't formally trained by the celebrated teachers. He was from a backwater tributary of the vast Roman empire. He had no pedigree, no prospects, and no purpose, in their eyes. Who was He to tell those who had spent their lives studying the Old Testament they were wrong?!

When He healed people miraculously, most of the recipients of this supernatural relief forgot Him. When He fed the hungry masses, they turned on Him when He said things they didn't like. Most of the folks who met Jesus used Him. They got what they wanted and walked away.

The longer He ministered, the more He angered people. After roughly three years of healing, teaching, loving, and leading, the religious authorities had had enough. They mustered a kangaroo court, scraped together some bad actors to bear false witness, and handed Him over to the Romans to crucify Him.

Yet, to the end of His life, Jesus loved. From the cross, He spoke words that I think most of us would find unfathomable. 'Father, forgive them, for they know not what they do' (Luke 23:34). Astonishing.

And He wasn't finished. They took Him down from the cross, buried Him and, on the third day, He walked out of the tomb. No other world religious leader did anything like that. Jesus' resurrection takes us to the heart of the matter when it comes to personal suffering and evil. The resurrection of Jesus proclaims that death, suffering, and all the evil in this world do not get the last word. Jesus does.

Knowing Jesus and knowing He is alive will make all the difference in our suffering. But the resurrection is not the end of the story.

BEDROCK TRUTH #5: THE HOLY SPIRIT IS STRONG

After Jesus ascended to the right hand of His Father (Acts 1:9, 2:33), He kept His promise to send the Holy Spirit (John 16:7). The Holy Spirit is the third person of the Trinity, fully God. He is a person, not a force (Acts 5:3, Eph. 4:30). He is the Spirit of God (Gen. 1:2) and the Spirit of Christ (Rom. 8:9). He is the Spirit of truth (John 14:17, 15:26) and the person of the Godhead who inspired the writers of Scripture to write what they wrote (2 Pet. 1:20).

The Lord Jesus continues His ministry in Christians' lives through the indwelling Holy Spirit (1 Cor. 15:45, 2 Cor. 3:16-18). Jesus, by the Spirit, is present with Christians every day. The Spirit dwells in them (Rom. 8:9; 2 Cor. 6:16). He is their advocate and their counselor. He prays when we do not know how to pray in our suffering (Rom. 8:26). He gives us weapons to fight the devil (Eph. 6:10-18).

Therefore, the Holy Spirit is present, active, and gentle in our suffering. We are not alone. That's one of our biggest fears when we suffer – being alone. 'Suffering is a given; suffering alone is intolerable.'[13] Christians never face the prospect of suffering alone. They have the strong Spirit, who will take from the riches of Christ (John 16:14-15), the supreme sufferer, and feed their souls when life falls apart.

In fact, the Spirit was 'made' for suffering, if I could put it like that. Of course, as God, the Spirit was never made. What I mean is that the Father and the Son send the Spirit to dwell in Christians in a fallen world. Dwelling in sinners in a sinful world – comforting them,

---

13. Johnson, *Hold Me Tight,* p. 24.

guiding them, drawing near to them – is the Spirit's natural environment.

He is not surprised by suffering or evil in our lives. He does not recoil from it. He draws near and comforts when everything else proves comfortless. He is most powerful when we feel most powerless.

HOPE FOR THE BROKEN

These five bedrock truths, drawn from Scripture, provide the only real foundation from which to face the problem of personal suffering and evil in our lives. As we examine various other solutions that have been proposed through the ages in the next chapter, we'll see that they are unsatisfying. Not just intellectually, but emotionally and spiritually. As we said at the outset, the subject of this book is not an intellectual curiosity. It is a visceral experience for every one of us. As we go along, I hope you'll see that God's answers to our deepest hurts not only satisfy the mind, they also comfort our broken hearts.

2

What Are Some Proposed Answers to This Question?

Maybe you've seen the bumper sticker, 'My karma ran over your dogma.' It's light-hearted but the slogan captures the mood of our age. Dogma is a bad word in our culture. When we say someone is dogmatic, we usually mean they are bigoted, intolerant, and close-minded. Hence the need, according to the bumper sticker, for such stray dogmas to be dispatched to the beyond by speeding karmas.

As an aside, don't miss the irony here. Karma is a *dogma* of Hinduism – a non-negotiable teaching! I'll echo an observation we made in the last chapter. A dismissive attitude towards dogmatic beliefs works fine when life is going well, but not so much when we suffer. We want relief. We want to know our pain is not meaningless. If there is a God, we want to know if He's there and if He'll help us when life hurts. In other words, suffering forces us to examine our dogmatic beliefs. We want to know if what we believe about whatever God or gods there may be is *true*.

In this chapter, we're going to examine solutions to the problem of personal suffering and evil offered by two major world religions. I am not a scholar of world religions by any means, but I think some representative statements make their views on these issues plain enough for us to evaluate. We'll also survey a recent bestselling book on the subject and its proposed remedy. As we work through these various teachings, I think you'll see that bumper sticker theology makes for a good laugh at the stoplight, but a poor guide for life. More importantly, we will learn that the answers given by those who practice religions other than Christianity (and by one philosopher we will analyze) do not stand up to scrutiny. Neither do they offer us much comfort for life's difficulties.

To be clear, I am not trying to be overly critical or unfair in my conclusions. World religions like the ones we'll examine are complex and I don't want to misrepresent them. A deep analysis of these complexities is beyond the scope of this book. Still, as I mentioned above, I think we can get a clear enough view of their teachings on this subject for our purposes.

I've divided this chapter into three main sections. First, we'll look at what a prominent Hindu teaches on this subject. Next, we'll look at the solution proposed by a scholar of Islam, the world's second largest religion. Third, we'll survey the work of philosopher and best-selling author Thomas Jay Oord.

HINDUISM, SUFFERING, AND EVIL

Hinduism is not, strictly speaking, a religion as we commonly understand that term. Shashi Tharoor, former Under Secretary General of the United Nations and a lifelong devout Hindu, explains, 'Hinduism is a civilization, not a dogma. There is no such thing as a Hindu heresy.' This is because, 'not even what one might think of as a basic tenet of any religion – belief in the existence of God – is a prerequisite in Hinduism.'[1]

While this teaching may sound foreign to Western ears, it is worked out in a multitude of ways in Hinduism. Despite requiring no fixed belief in God, Tharoor is quick to point out that Hindus do have *some* fixed beliefs. Chief among them is the doctrine of reincarnation (or *punarjanmam*). He goes on to explain that their under-standing of reincarnation is essential to Hinduism's answer for the question of personal suffering and evil. 'The idea of reincarnation, emerging from the endless cycle of birth and rebirth, is basic to Hinduism ... this

---

1. Shashi Tharoor, *Why I Am a Hindu* (Victoria, Australia: Scribe Publications, 2019), p. 8, for both references.

cycle of birth, death and rebirth is known as Samsara, and it is a belief that addresses one of the central challenges facing every believer in God – if God is all-knowing, all-seeing, all-compassionate and merciful, why does He permit so much suffering, pain, inequality and inequity to bedevil His creations?'[2]

Tharoor confesses that this teaching seemed very unsatisfying to him at first blush. 'I always considered this deeply unfair: why should a human being, conscious only of himself in his present life, have to suffer for wrongs he does not recollect and misdeeds he has no memory of having committed in previous lives of which he is unaware?'[3] Indeed, this may be *the* central problem with the doctrine of reincarnation.

But Tharoor believes his questions are not as challenging as they first appear. To see why, he encourages the reader to stop thinking of God as an 'old man in a white beard looking down benevolently at you from the heavens, listening to your prayers and interceding when He [sees] fit.'[4] Leaving aside Tharoor's parody of a standard view of God, he tells us that he resolved his doubts about reincarnation by adopting an impersonal view of God. He encourages his readers to do likewise.

2. Ibid., pp. 89-90.
3. Ibid., p. 90.
4. Ibid.

'If you stopped thinking of God [in a personal fashion], however, but saw God in everyone and everything, in the bad and the good, in the unfair as well as the just, as impersonal cosmic force that just *is* – then you can come to terms with the world's tragedies as well as its joys.'[5] In sum, Tharoor wants us to see that reincarnation is not unfair. It's just the way things are. If we accept this, then we can accept the tragedies of life.

Another dogma of Hinduism (which is part and parcel of the doctrine of reincarnation) is karma. Again, Tharoor explains this connection well. 'The idea of reincarnation is related to that of *karma*, or action – the accumulated actions of your life. So the very circumstances of your birth – the home, the place, the nation and the opportunities into which you are born – are determined by your soul's actions in its previous incarnation.'[6] Here is the pattern, then. Our karma from our previous lives determines our reincarnation.

Given this basic sketch of some key Hindu beliefs, we can ask again, 'Yes, but do these doctrines help us when we suffer?' I don't think so, for a number of reasons.

First, it is apparent that we cannot know what we did in a previous life, as Tharoor admits. But if that is the case, then how can we know that our present suffering

---

5. Ibid., pp. 90-91.
6. Ibid., p. 91; emphasis original.

is a result of prior actions, as karma requires? Stated in another way, the doctrine of karma seems less like an *explanation* and more like just an *admission of ignorance.*

Second, Tharoor's solution to this obvious problem – thinking of God as an impersonal force that we should see in all things, good and evil – is not much help either. An impersonal force doesn't care about good or evil. Indeed, it *can't* care about such things. But if that's the case, then how can karma determine our reincarnation? After all, karma is supposed to be *just* – we get what we deserve based on our actions. But, again, an impersonal force does not and cannot care about justice. Tharoor's proposal has offered us a deeply conflicted view about the real meaning of the universe.

More broadly, if God is an impersonal force, then it's difficult to see how we can even distinguish between good and evil, suffering and happiness. Such moral concepts presuppose a moral lawgiver, not an impersonal force. Tharoor's answer leaves us with no solid ground on which to stand to distinguish between good and evil. Instead, what he offers us is a rather merciless worldview.

Of course, very few people will want this kind of merciless, impersonal universe. Returning to our original point, all of us want to know *why* we suffer. Stated another way, we may claim we just accept that suffering and evil are the way things are, but few of us can live that answer out consistently.

ISLAM, SUFFERING, AND EVIL

The polar opposite of Hinduism is Islam. By some accounts, Islam is the fastest growing religion in the world. The hallmark of this religion is its rigid commitment to monotheism, the conviction that there is only one God, Allah. Unlike Hinduism, Islam prescribes in very concrete terms what one must do and believe. Therefore, we will look at one Islamic scholar's answer to the question of personal suffering and evil.

At the outset, we should note that the Qur'an (Islam's holy book) does not address suffering and evil in the kind of detail we find in the Bible. One reason for this absence is that the main purpose of the Qur'an is to teach Muslims Allah's will. Unlike the Bible, which presents much of its material in narrative form, a large part of the Qur'an consists of direct commands. As one scholar explains, 'The Qur'an is almost entirely *hortatory*. Although it contains narrative, nearly every story is told as part of an argument or exhortation.'[7] As a result, the Qur'an does not wrestle with the problem of personal

---

7.   Ida Glaser, 'Qur'anic Challenges for the Bible Reader' in *The Enduring Authority of the Christian Scriptures*, ed. D. A. Carson (Grand Rapids, MI: William B. Eerdmans Publishing Company, 2016), p. 1027; emphasis original.

suffering and evil in the same way as the Bible because these twin evils are simply Allah's will – end of story.

A helpful summary of an Islamic viewpoint on these issues comes from Dr. Muzammil H. Siddiqi, former president of the Islamic Society of North America. He writes:

> The Qur'an tells us that good, evil and whatever happens in this world happens by Allah's Will ... sufferings occur to teach us that we must adhere to Allah's natural and moral laws. It is sometimes to punish those who violate Allah's natural or moral laws. It is to test our faith in Allah and to test our commitment to human values and charity. Whenever we encounter suffering we should ask ourselves, 'Have we broken any law of Allah?' Let us study the cause of the problem and use the corrective methods. 'Could it be a punishment?' Let us repent and ask forgiveness and reform our ways. 'Could it be a test and trial for us?' Let us work hard to pass this test. Believers face the sufferings with prayers, repentance and good deeds.[8]

Siddiqi's first sentence reinforces what we said about the Muslim view of how the Qur'an functions in Islamic life, while his three questions represent a practical

---

8. Dr. Muzammil H. Siddiqi, 'Why Does Allah Allow Suffering and Evil in the World?,' https://aboutislam.net/counseling/ask-the-scholar/muslim-creed/why-does-allah-allow-suffering-and-evil-in-the-world/, accessed January 22, 2024.

outworking of Islamic theology as it relates to Allah's will and our suffering.

We need to pause and appreciate Dr. Siddiqi's answer. For Christians, his queries could be very much appropriate to ask in some contexts. For example, Christians believe that some of the suffering people undergo is a result of disobeying God's law. Christians also believe that one purpose of suffering is to test our faith.

Even with these similarities, the differences between an Islamic understanding of suffering and evil like the one above and the biblical teaching on this subject are important. Let's focus our attention on what might be the biggest difference – how the Bible presents the relationship between God's sovereignty and our free will, versus the Qur'an's teaching.

Above, Siddiqi told us that Allah's unqualified sovereignty is the chief cause of our sufferings and evil. Given this baseline, he then instructs sufferers to do any number of things – repent, reform, or patiently endure the test. But here's the question that highlights the difference between the Bible's teaching and that of the Qur'an: 'Why should we do these things when we suffer?' Siddiqi answers, 'To teach us that we must adhere to Allah's natural and moral laws.' That reply raises another question. 'What is the goal of my obedience to these laws?' Presumably, the answer is, 'To obtain eternal bliss and the end of our suffering.' Here a major problem arises for Islam. Authoritative interpretations of the Qur'an teach that even if one does what is required (such as those things Siddiqi outlined above), Allah could still condemn them to everlasting punishment. In other words, on the Qur'anic view, even if we do what Siddiqi prescribes when we suffer, it may not matter in the end, because there is still the risk that we will suffer for eternity.

An example from the *ahadith*, which are a vast collection of sayings by Muhammed and his companions that function as a living tradition – an interpretive grid for the Qur'an – illustrates this conundrum. In one *hadith*, Sahih Al-Bukhari, 8:593, we read,

> And by Allah, a person among you (or a man) may do deeds of the people of the Fire till there is only a cubit or an arm-breadth distance between him and the Fire, but then that writing (which Allah has ordered the angel to write) precedes, and he does the deeds of the people of Paradise and enters it; and a man may do the deeds of the people of Paradise till there is only a cubit or two between him and Paradise, and then that writing precedes and he does the deeds of the people of the Fire and enters it.[9]

---

9. Cited in James R. White, *What Every Christian Needs to Know About the Qur'an* (Minneapolis, MN: Bethany House Publishers, 2013), p. 156.

The key phrase here is 'that writing precedes,' which refers to the prior decree of Allah. So, this text teaches Allah could decree that someone leads an immoral life ('do the deeds of Fire') and then, at the last moment, this person could be saved from everlasting torment because Allah so willed it. More alarmingly, the reverse is also the case: Allah could decree that someone leads a moral life ('do the deeds of the people of Paradise') and then, at the last moment, this person could go into everlasting torment because Allah so willed it.

Given this view of Allah's sovereignty, one scholar rightly concludes that Allah's decree is 'utterly capricious,' which 'empties it of moral or ethical meaning.'[10] How can we believe Allah is good if he exercises his sovereignty in such an arbitrary fashion?

This kind of uncertainty is no help to us when we suffer. Suppose someone you meet has experienced all kinds of calamities in his life. Finally, he dies from a terrible, wasting disease. Is there any hope for him, given what Islam teaches? *Possibly.* And that's the problem – there is no *guarantee* that his good works, like following Siddiqi's advice, result in his entrance into paradise. Instead, his suffering might get even worse.

This brief summary of Siddiqi's answer helps us to see that what we believe about what happens after we

---

10. Ibid.

die exercises considerable influence over how we live – and suffer – in this life. On the one hand, if life ends when we die, then all is meaningless in the present, as we saw with the naturalistic worldview in chapter 1. On the other hand, Islamic teaching tells us that we may do all Siddiqi and others tell us to do, but none of that may matter in the end. We end up suffering *even more* after we die.

In stark contrast to these options, the Bible teaches that God permits us to suffer for greater purposes, some of which He reveals and some of which He does not (we'll discuss this point in more detail below). While we may not know all His purposes, He assures us of His love and promises Christians that they can be *sure* their suffering will end. This is because God's decree, according to the Bible, is not capricious or arbitrary.

In addition, on the biblical view, a Christian's admittance to heaven is not based on anything he or she does but is a gift of God's sheer grace, offered to us in Jesus. He lived a perfect life in our place and died an atoning death for our sins. Therefore, in the Christian worldview, Jesus accomplishes everything for those who believe in Him. As a result of His work for us, we can be *certain* of our eternal destiny (since it all depends on God's grace), which gives us certain hope in the midst of our present difficulties.

So, we don't have to throw up our hands and say with Tharoor, 'I suffer and that's the way it is.' No, the Bible tells us God has good purposes for our suffering and, if we believe in Jesus, we can be assured they will end. Nor do we have to follow Siddiqi and submit ourselves to the will of an arbitrary deity, whose decree might nullify whatever we do to relieve our suffering in this life or in the next. Instead, if we turn to Jesus in faith, we can avoid both of these unappealing options.

A POPULAR SOLUTION

Finally, we come to Thomas Jay Oord's book, *God Can't!*, which offers a very different perspective than the previous two worldviews (or the orthodox Christian worldview, for that matter) on personal suffering and evil. By 'orthodox,' I mean what most Christians have taught and believed over the centuries. Since he is a professing Christian, and this book is written from a Christian viewpoint, Oord's proposal deserves our attention, especially since it represents (in my view) a sweeping departure from what the Bible teaches.

Oord is an open theist, which means he denies central beliefs that Christians have always taught. His view is called 'open' theism because, in rough terms, it teaches that God is 'open' to different outcomes, depending on the choices of His human creatures. One of the basic teachings of open theism, then, is that God does not know the future because He *cannot* know it. Why? Because God does not know what humans will choose.

Based on this view of God's sovereignty (or lack thereof), Oord leaves no doubt about his understanding of God's relationship to suffering and evil. 'Let me get right to the first idea we need: God can't prevent abuse, tragedy, and evil. You read it right: God *can't*. A loving God simply cannot do some things.' However, he adds this qualification. 'To put it more precisely, God can't prevent evil *singlehandedly*.'[11]

Oord emphasizes 'singlehandedly' because he argues that we work *with* God to prevent evil. He describes the connection between God's sovereignty and human choice as 'indispensable love synergy.'[12] What does he mean by these terms? 'God *needs* us and others for love to win. Our contributions are *essential* to establishing overall well-being. Without cooperation, God *cannot* attain these positive outcomes.'[13]

Oord goes on to contrast the indispensable love synergy view with what he calls the 'all God' interpretation of God's control over evil. He explains (or, rather, caricatures) the classic

---

11. Thomas Jay Oord, *God Can't: How to Believe in God and Love After Tragedy, Abuse, and Other Evils* (n.p.: SacraSage Press, 2019), p. 17, emphasis original.
12. Ibid., p. 142; emphasis original.
13. Ibid.

understanding of God's sovereignty this way. 'God controls everyone and everything. We're puppets … controlled people don't "obey". They're wind-up toys.'[14]

The essence of Oord's conception of God is that because He is essentially love[15] and love is always 'self-giving and others-empowering,'[16] it follows that divine love 'gives freedom to complex creatures like you and me.'[17] As a result, God can't prevent moral evils because it would be unloving for a supremely loving being to override His creatures' free will.

We should recognize that there is nothing new in Oord's view. Nor is there anything new in the view for which I am arguing – Oord's so-called 'all God' view. Oord's solution has been tried before, in various forms, and found wanting every time. But, since his book is influential, I'll offer a few reasons we should reject Oord's position.

OORD'S CONFUSIONS

First, Oord's claims that God 'needs' us and that He 'cannot' prevent evil without our help make God dependent on His creatures to accomplish His purposes.

---

14. Ibid., p. 145.
15. Ibid., p. 28.
16. Ibid.
17. Ibid., p. 27.

But a god dependent on his creation is simply not the God of the Bible. Oord recognizes that his view is radical,[18] but it's more than radical. It's a complete recasting of the Christian view of God. Whatever else this view is, it stretches the limits of credulity to call it Christian, in any meaningful sense.

Second, as I mentioned above, Oord caricatures the historic Christian understanding of the relationship between God's sovereignty and our free will. The Bible does not teach we are 'wind-up toys' or 'puppets.' Instead, God's Word teaches two truths – God is sovereign and we have the ability to choose freely *according to our desires* (see Matthew 11:25-30 and Acts 2:23 for representative examples of the Bible's teaching on this relationship). In philosophical terms, this view is a species of *compatibilism* – our choices are compatible with God's absolute sovereignty.

In the Bible, humans enjoy *qualified* free will. Theologians have explained it this way. When it comes to the exercise of our wills, we should distinguish between the liberty of *spontaneity* and the liberty of *indifference*.[19] The former simply means we choose according to our desires – some people prefer vanilla ice cream, some

---

18. Ibid., p. 142.

19. See Robert L. Reymond, *A New Systematic Theology of the Christian Faith*, 2nd ed. (Nashville: Thomas Nelson, 1998), p. 372, for this characterization.

people dislike the color blue, etc. The latter means that the human will is utterly and totally free – it is not determined by anything from within or without. Oord's view requires that we think of the human will in terms of the liberty of indifference. This interpretation is both unbiblical and indefensible on its own terms.

First, the Bible never teaches that humans have unrestricted free will, as Oord's argument requires. Theologian and philosopher John Frame explains, 'There is no passage [in Scripture] that can be construed to mean that the human will is independent of God's plan and of the rest of the human personality.'[20] So Oord's characterization of human free will is not biblical.

Second, even if you don't agree with the Bible's teaching on these matters, Oord's argument has a glaring problem. Recall he told us that God can't prevent suffering and evil because, if God overrides our free will, that would make us 'wind-up toys.'

Pejorative language aside, we should notice that Oord's overall argument is designed to avoid *meticulous* divine providence at all costs.[21] This is the view that I

---

20. John M. Frame, *No Other God: A Response to Open Theism* (Phillipsburg, NJ: P&R Publishing, 2001), p. 125.

21. See Greg Welty, 'Open Theism, Risk-Taking, and the Problem of Evil,' in *Philosophical Essays Against Open Theism*, ed. Benjamin H. Arbour (New York and London: Routledge, 2019), p. 149, for the distinction between meticulous and general providence.

hold, which, in broad terms, teaches that God controls everything in the universe, including our suffering and evil – what Oord chides as the 'All God' interpretation of God's control. He tells us that this understanding of God's sovereign control over suffering and evil would make us 'puppets.' Accordingly, Oord's view requires that God permits these things because He can't accomplish His purposes without the cooperation of our free will choices.

But his rigid commitment to the 'love synergy view' of God's sovereignty has some major problems. For example, suppose God knows someone is about to murder another person. God has a choice in this moment: intervene and prevent the murder or permit it to happen. Oord would claim it is unloving for God to override the free will of the murderer and therefore permits the murder to happen. God *can't* stop the murder. For Oord, then, the *general* reason God permits us to suffer is that He values preserving our free will over intervening to prevent some evil. Oord is forced to this conclusion because he does not want to admit God's sovereignty is meticulous in any instance.

Here's the difficulty with this kind of thinking. Since Oord writes as a Christian, he knows there are multitudes of instances in the Bible where God *does* intervene – where He exercises meticulous control in governing the world. This being the case, preserving our free will cannot be the *general* reason God permits evil to happen, since He *has*, in fact, prevented moral or natural evils on many occasions. Therefore, His reasons for doing so are *specific* and not *general*, as Oord assumes. Stated in plain terms, all divine providence is meticulous and not general. As a result, Oord's argument does not stand up to scrutiny, even on its own terms.

Now, the more perplexing question raised by our analysis of Oord's view is, 'Why does God choose to intervene in some instances and not in others?' Without wanting to be callous or trite, the Bible's answer is that He has a good reason for His choices. I'll try to flesh out why this is true as we conclude this chapter.

No Sovereignty, No Solution to Personal Evil and Suffering

The proposals we have examined reveal our need to understand the relationship between God's sovereignty and our suffering. One author offers a helpful way to understand this connection. In a nutshell, he argues that, since the Bible teaches that God controls all things meticulously *and* places high value on our moral choices (free will in a qualified sense), then if God chooses to intervene or not to intervene at any given point, He does so for a good reason.[22]

---

22. Ibid., p. 150.

That answer may make you want to throw this book down (if you haven't wanted to already!). But this answer brings us face to face with *the* main issue when we suffer: will we trust God when we don't understand His ways? Will we believe He has good reasons we cannot know?

ONE MISSIONARY'S TESTIMONY

What if we admit that God has good reasons for our suffering? Naturally, we would then ask, 'Does it work? Does believing God has good reasons for my suffering that I cannot know help me when I suffer?' These are valid questions. So, by way of answer, let me share an example of someone who trusted that God had reasons for her suffering she did not understand, to demonstrate that believing this truth does, in fact, work.

I am thinking of missionary Helen Roseveare. Her testimony is powerful, heartbreaking, and hope-filled. As we have said over and over, personal suffering and evil are not academic concerns. They are visceral realities. Her story illustrates the simple truth that what we said above – that God has good reasons for the evil and suffering we undergo – is not just an academic solution we can live with. It's a truth we can't live without.

Roseveare was a Cambridge-trained doctor who dedicated her life to serving some of the poorest people in the world. She was in the Congo in 1964 when civil war broke out. Priests and missionaries were ruthlessly slaughtered, along with about 250,000 Africans. Here is her riveting account of what happened to her during this time.

> I could not cancel it out, as though it had never been, the memory of that awful night of 29 October 1964 … The soldiers came. Naked beams of light stabbed the night, and I was alone. They found me, dragged me to my feet, struck me over head and shoulders, flung me on the ground, kicked me, dragged me to my feet only to strike me again – the sickening, searing pain of a broken tooth, a mouth full of sticky blood, my glasses gone. Beyond sense, numb with horror and unknown fear, driven, dragged, pushed back to my own house, yelled at, insulted, cursed.[23]

She cried out in her soul, 'My God, my God, why have You forgotten me, forsaken me? … alone, oh how alone!'[24] While few of us have ever experienced anything like this violence, all of us can relate to her cry – we feel alone in our suffering, forsaken.

Yet, amid this wracking horror, she recounts, 'Suddenly Christ had been there. No vision, no voice, but His very real presence. He spoke to my heart: "They're

---

23. Helen Roseveare, *He Gave Us a Valley* (Fearn, Tain, Ross-shire: Christian Focus Publications, 2006), p. 35.

24. Ibid.

not fighting you: these blows, all this wickedness, is against Me. All I ask of you is the loan of your body. Will you share with Me one hour in My sufferings for these who need My love through you?"'[25]

She continues, 'Two contradictory reactions possessed my heart in that instance. How could He ask me to love these wicked, evil brutes? And yet, how could He, almighty creator God as He was, condescend to ask me to do Him a favour? ... He was presenting me with His need and offering me the inestimable privilege of satisfying that need – the loan of my body.'[26]

Roseveare believed that God was almighty, that He was condescending to her in this moment. An almighty God, by definition, could have prevented this trauma from happening to her. Knowing this, she could have simply given up her faith in Jesus and said, 'No loving God would ever permit this to happen to me.'

Instead, she sensed God speaking to her heart. She went so far as to call her extreme suffering a 'privilege.' Can you imagine reacting like that if you were in her place?

I've been a Christian for over twenty years and I admit, I have a hard time believing that I would share Roseveare's faith if this happened to me. But her trust in

---

25. Ibid., p. 36.
26. Ibid.

an almighty God gave her unshakable confidence that there were at least two reasons for suffering: to share in the fellowship of Jesus' sufferings, as the Bible promises will happen (see Philippians 1:29 and 3:10) and to show the love of Jesus in precisely the same way He loves – by loving her enemies.

Her testimony demonstrates that believing God has reasons for our suffering, even if we never know all of them, makes all the difference when our worst fears come true. We need to be clear, though. Just because God has reasons for permitting such atrocities does not make them or those who perpetrate them any less evil. Even Roseveare called her attackers what they were: evil brutes. All that to say, God *permitting* evil is not the same thing at all as God *condoning* evil or expecting those who endure it to sit by passively. Evil must be named for what it is and resisted with all the resources we have available to us.

I also think it's important to understand that Roseveare wouldn't want us to think she is an exceptional case of believing in God in unimaginable circumstances. She goes to great lengths in her book to make it clear that she is not some kind of 'super believer.' In fact, she struggled with going back to serve in Africa after the violence she endured.[27] But she did return. And her story

---

27. Ibid., pp. 50-51.

shows us that God can help ordinary people like us, even when we suffer in ways we never thought possible. In sum, she wants us to see that her faith can be ours too.

We have seen that various worldviews and religions cannot really help us answer the question of why we suffer so much in this life. The Bible can and does. Countless people throughout the ages have reached out with the trembling hand of faith and found the strong grasp of God's hand, as it were, when life falls apart, just like Roseveare. If we reach out in faith, we will meet the same God, the only One who can offer us an answer to our questions, even if we never understand His ways fully.

3

What Does the Bible Teach Us About Depression, Anxiety, and Fear?

A Poet's Struggle

One of the outstanding English poets of the eighteenth century was a man by the name of William Cowper (pronounced *Cooper*). He was also a parishioner of John Newton, the former slave trader turned pastor, who wrote probably the most well-known hymn of all time, 'Amazing Grace.' Born into the aristocracy of that time, Cowper battled crippling depression throughout his life, attempting suicide on multiple occasions. Yet even though he suffered from what we would now call clinical depression, Cowper managed to write beautiful hymns expressing faith and trust in Jesus.

His story does not have a happy ending. Cowper died inconsolably depressed in March of 1800. His lifelong struggle reminds us that faithful Christians can wrestle with depression, anxiety, and fear. Many people are under the mistaken impression that if you become a Christian, your problems disappear overnight. The testimony of men like Cowper and countless other believers over the centuries would beg to differ.

Today, depression and anxiety are on the rise in the United States. For example, a recent Gallup poll surveyed a sample of over 100,000 adults and at least 29 per cent reported being diagnosed with some form of depression. This is the largest percentage since researchers began tracking the data in 2015.[1]

Even if these statistics are inflated, we all know people who suffer from anxiety and depression. In other words, these are widespread problems. But, as we pointed out earlier, those of us in the West probably enjoy the most material abundance of any civilization in the history of humankind.

These two sets of facts do not seem to make any sense. How can we have so much and still remain so unhappy? I think Jesus gives us a ready answer. He said, 'One's life does not consist in the abundance of his possessions' (Luke 12:15). We can have everything and still have nothing, in other words. We need something more than earthly treasures and comfort.

---

1. Dan Witters, 'U.S. Depression Rates Reach New Highs,' https://news.gallup.com/poll/505745/depression-rates-reach-new-highs.aspx, accessed August 21, 2024.

In this chapter, we will try to understand, from the Bible's perspective, why we suffer with depression, anxiety, and fear. We'll then mine the Scriptures to see what they say to us amid these painful realities.

Four Alienations

A bedrock truth from chapter 1 is the fact that sin is real. Going deeper, Adam's sin had massive consequences. We need to understand four of them, as they will be indispensable for our discussion that follows.

Numerous theologians have identified four alienations that took place when Adam plunged the human race into sin and misery. First, and most importantly, man was alienated *from God*. This is why our first parents hid themselves in shame and terror when they heard God approaching (Gen. 3:8). Peaceful fellowship with their creator had been replaced by a fractured relationship.

Second, Adam's sin alienates us *from nature*. This is at least one reason why we experience natural disasters, wild animals who will kill us, and a host of other tragedies in the natural world. Humans were meant to be God's stewards of nature, cultivating it for His glory. Instead, nature resists man's attempts at godly stewardship because of Adam's sin (Gen. 3:17-19).

Third, people are now alienated from *each other*. When God questions the fallen pair, for the first time ever we witness a broken relationship between humans. Adam tries to shift the blame to God and then Eve, who, in turn, tries to shift the blame to the serpent (Gen. 3:12-13). A relationship of love, trust, and integrity is gone between the first husband and wife. In its place, we find suspicion, self-interest, and deception. Sound familiar?

The terrible consequences of this alienation come to fruition quickly. Scarcely a chapter later, we witness the first murder in human history, an instance of fratricide (Gen. 4:8). Since the fall, humans are hostile to each other because we are alienated from each other by sin.

Finally, sin alienates man *from himself.* This is important to grasp for the purposes of this chapter. We were not meant to experience depression, anxiety, and fear. Where did they come from? Consider God's promise of hardship to Adam in Genesis 3:19: 'By the sweat of your face you shall eat bread, till you return to the ground, for out of it you were taken; for you are dust, and to dust you shall return.' Put in more modern terms, God is telling Adam that his life on earth is going to be hard.

Depression, anxiety, and fear, therefore, are not natural. They were not emotions that humankind had before the fall. They are invaders, intruders, usurpers. They result from man's alienation from himself.

Of course, the biblical view of these psychological problems is miles apart from what behavioral scientists think today. Modern psychology, in large part, takes the evolutionary worldview for granted. Therefore, depression, anxiety, and fear are *solely* physiological realities. This follows from a consistent naturalistic worldview. On this understanding, either our minds are not real (because mind is not matter) or mind arises from matter – and that is the end of the matter.

By contrast, the Bible recognizes that there is a physiological component to depression, anxiety, and fear. At times, the physiological factor may be the most important, in fact. But the reason we experience these painful issues cannot be explained at a wholly biological level. According to God's Word, we are body and soul, not body only. The Bible's teaching about humanity opens a far better path to understand our psychological problems.

To be clear, if we are depressed, or anxious, or fearful, what we're experiencing may require medical attention. Researchers have distinguished between *clinical* and *situational* depression, for example. The difference between the two is more of degree than kind and both can be serious. Situational depression may require the help of a medical professional while clinical depression most certainly does.

We also need to be clear that psychology is what is known as a 'soft science.' This is not a term of derision; it simply means that psychology and psychiatry are not the same as the 'hard sciences,' such as biology, physiology, chemistry, etc. The soft sciences, in other words, cannot quantify the data in the same way as the hard sciences. So, of necessity, the conclusions of the soft sciences are far more provisional than those of the hard sciences.

For example, if you suffer from acid reflux, there are a host of well-tested, proven causes for this condition. Every human stomach functions the same way, allowing doctors to prescribe certain regimens to lessen or cure the symptoms. Of course, acid reflux might be a result of stress, anxiety, or a host of other psychological problems. But the presenting symptoms of acid reflux are primarily physiological and uniform, regardless of how patients get them.

By contrast, psychological afflictions like depression, anxiety, and fear differ widely from person to person. Our stomachs share the same basic biology; our psychology does not.

All that to say, a major weakness of the evolutionary worldview, as it informs discussions about the issues we are studying, is that it makes what might be a mind/body problem into a body problem *only*. And therefore, this worldview tends to believe that given the right pharmaceutical therapy, we can relieve most of the symptoms of depression, anxiety, and fear.

For example, one evolutionary thinker offers this naïve and overly-optimistic treatment plan for our anxiety and depression. 'Take two of whatever neuropharmacology prescribes. If you don't feel better in the morning … or three weeks from now, switch to another one.'[2] This 'prescription' is not only naïve, it is simplistic. The data on 'whatever neuropharmacology prescribes' certainly do not suggest that medication will make all our problems go away, no matter how many different regimens we try. No, we humans – and our problems – are far too complex for a glass of water and a pill to fix.

Basics of Biblical Psychology

Before we go further, we must get some basics of biblical psychology clear. As we mentioned above, the biblical worldview tells us that man is body and soul (Gen. 2:7; Matt. 10:28). These two are integrated such that a whole person is not simply a soul trapped in a body (as Plato taught and many Eastern religions teach), nor is man simply a 'meat machine' (the evolutionary view). Instead, we are *embodied souls*. The two were never meant to be separated.

The Bible also teaches that the center of man's being, as it were, is his heart. Not the physical organ,

---

2. Alex Rosenberg, *The Atheist's Guide to Reality: Enjoying Life Without Illusions* (New York: W.W. Norton Co., 2011), p. 282.

but who we are at our core – the real 'us.' We use the word 'heart' in a similar sense in our culture. For example, Genesis 6:5 pronounces, 'The LORD saw that the wickedness of man was great in the earth, and that every intention of the thoughts of his *heart* was only evil continually.' This verse is telling us that our hearts – our innermost being – are corrupt. Jesus echoes this understanding when He says, 'What comes out of a person is what defiles him. For from within, out of the *heart* of man, come evil thoughts, sexual immorality, theft, murder, adultery, coveting, wickedness, deceit, sensuality, envy, slander, pride, foolishness' (Mark 7:20-22; emphasis mine).

So, we are body and soul, an integrated union, and our hearts are the center of who we are. Therefore, our hearts and souls are integrated as well. Therefore, when the Bible speaks of our hearts, it means our inner life – our emotions, our affections, our will, our intellect. Our heart desires express the 'soul' of our souls, if I could put it like that.

Notice how the biblical view of humanity differs from culture's view of humanity. Why is this important to recognize? Because the culture around us tells us to 'follow our hearts.' The assumption here is that we have our intellect on one hand and our heart – our feelings – on the other. The two are separated. Therefore, we can think through something rationally, but eventually we just need to follow our hearts.

Returning to an observation we made in the last chapter, notice how this separation between the head and the heart reflects a subtle form of oneness thinking. Feelings are superior to intellect – we need to empty our minds, remember? For a lot of people, empty minds plus full hearts is the way to go.

As with all ideas, this head/heart separation has consequences. In my work as a pastor, I've witnessed firsthand the disastrous results of people 'following their hearts.' I've seen spouses abandon their families for another lover because they were 'following their hearts.' Even with the emotional pain that comes from accepting the pop axiom that we should follow our hearts, this kind of thinking is so ingrained that it seems almost blasphemous to question it.

But question it we must. If we want to get real help with our depression, anxiety, and fear, we need to have a right understanding of who we are as humans, which the Bible provides. All unbiblical divisions or confusions need to be set aside, or we'll never experience the freedom, joy, and peace God intends for His creatures.

DEPRESSION AND ANXIETY

Now that we have a thumbnail sketch of biblical psychology, let's consider depression. Why do we get depressed? There are so many reasons, aren't there? Maybe you've lost your job, your friends, or your spouse. Maybe you've wanted to get married and that hasn't happened. Maybe you struggle financially. Maybe you have been a 'glass half-empty' person your whole life. The list of reasons for depression is endless.

Maybe it's more serious for you. Maybe you suffer from clinical depression. You didn't ask for it and it comes without warning. It is a serious issue. As I said at the outset, if you are experiencing clinical depression, seek the help of a medical professional immediately.

Whether clinical or situational, the Bible speaks to all kinds of depression. If you open the book of Psalms and you're depressed, you will meet some wonderful fellow travelers. This is why the Reformer John Calvin called the psalms 'the anatomy of all the parts of the soul.'[3] The words of these ancient writers capture the whole breadth of the human experience, including depression.

Here's a tiny sampling. 'My soul also is greatly troubled. But you, O LORD – how long?' (Ps. 6:3). 'How long must I take counsel in my soul and have sorrow in my heart all the day?' (Ps. 13:2). 'For my soul is full of troubles' (Ps. 88:3). We could multiply many times over the anguished cries of the psalmists like these.

---

3. John Calvin, Preface to the *Commentary on Psalms 1-35* (Grand Rapids: Baker Books, 2003), vol. IV: xxxvii.

Depression, then, is something that has afflicted not just non-Christians, but Christians since the fall. We need to emphasize this point because there is a pervasive (and perverse) understanding of the gospel today that needs correcting. Sometimes, well-meaning folk have presented the gospel along these lines. 'If you believe in Jesus, He will take away all your troubles.' That is true in an ultimate sense, but radically false in a proximate, day-to-day sense. Certainly, when we come to Christ, everything changes (John 3:3; 2 Cor. 3:16). But that does not mean that we are instantly transformed into all that we will be in Christ.

No, as the Bible makes clear, believers will always wrestle with the painful effects of the fall in this life, including depression. The *fact* of depression is one thing. It's widespread. But what about the *reason* for depression and anxiety? Why would a loving God allow us to suffer such things?

The biblical answers will challenge us. They do not conform to popular opinion. They are the polar opposite of conventional wisdom. They are hard to hear. But they are true. And they will help us on the dark road of depression and anxiety. Let's look at a few of them.

According to Scripture, the main reason we suffer with depression and anxiety is the sin of Adam. We touched on this fact over the past few chapters; now we need to dive deeper.

COVENANT: A FORGOTTEN AND IMPORTANT TRUTH

All people sinned when Adam sinned. Paul makes this crystal clear in Romans 5:12: 'Therefore, just as sin came into the world through one man, and death through sin, and so death spread to all men because all sinned.' Paul is reminding us that Adam was the covenant head of the human race. The concept of 'covenant head' requires further explanation.

Covenant is how God relates to His creatures and it's the central, unifying storyline of the Bible. What is a covenant in the Bible? One scholar explains that it is a 'legal agreement between two parties that is ratified by certain rituals that emphasize the binding nature of the agreement.'[4] So a covenant is not merely a contract or an agreement. It is an indissoluble bond.

The very idea of covenant once again highlights the difference between biblical Christianity and every other religion. God binds Himself to keep His promise to save a people for Himself, not because of anything they *do*, but because of who He *is* (Isa. 45:4, 48:9; Heb. 6:13-14). Salvation in Jesus is a result of God keeping His covenant promises to His creatures. He saves them by grace alone because He does not lie to them. What He promises,

---

4. Richard P. Belcher, Jr., *The Fulfillment of the Promises of God: An Explanation of Covenant Theology* (Fearn, Ross-shire: Christian Focus Publications, 2020), p. 18.

He obligates Himself to do, even when His creatures fail on their end. The essence of covenant from God's perspective is, in this sense, one-sided. By entering into covenant with us, God does everything necessary for our salvation.

On the human side, our failure to keep God's covenant stretches back to the dawn of creation. God placed Adam in the garden and gave him a command: 'Do not eat of this tree' (see Gen. 2:17). He promised Adam and his descendants everlasting life for obedience and everlasting death for disobedience. This first covenant was called the *covenant of works*. Adam had to obey to inherit eternal life. We know how the story ends. He failed miserably.

So, God made a second covenant, called the *covenant of grace*, which was administered in successive times from Adam to Noah to Abraham to Moses to David to Jesus. Jesus perfectly fulfilled the covenant of works by obeying God's commands. His perfect obedience becomes ours when we place our faith in Him, since He is the covenant head of the covenant of grace. One covenant of works, which Adam broke and plunged us all into sin. One covenant of grace, different administrations, with Jesus as the head. That's the biblical storyline in a nutshell.[5]

---

5. To be clear, the phrases 'covenant of works' and 'covenant of grace' do not appear in the Bible. But they summarize what the Bible teaches on these subjects.

You may be asking yourself, 'What in the world does this have to do with depression and anxiety?' Everything. You see, as the verse from Romans cited above makes clear, Adam was a covenant representative – a covenant head – of the whole human race when he sinned. The disastrous results of his choice affected all of us.

As a result, the first reason we experience depression and anxiety, even if they are not a result of our sin, is because they are the result of *Adam's* sin. He brought us all down with him and that's why we get down. Because of the fall, depression and anxiety are part of the operating system, as it were, in this world.

The second reason we experience anxiety and depression may come as a result of our own sin. 'The way of the treacherous is their ruin' (Prov. 13:15). Or, as the old King James translates this verse, 'The way of transgressors is hard.'

It may not seem very kind to speak this way. After all, so much of the depression and anxiety that plagues us seems to come out of nowhere or is caused by something other than our own sin. I completely agree. But we do need to at least consider the fact that, for some of us, our sin has led to the way we feel.

For example, if you have sex with a lot of different people, God may convict you of this sin by allowing you to feel guilt and shame, leading to depression. I chose sexual sin as an example because of the astonishing way the Bible describes this kind of sin. 'Flee from sexual immorality. Every other sin a person commits is outside the body, but the sexually immoral person sins against his own body' (1 Cor. 6:18). All sin deserves God's wrath. But there is something about sexual sin that affects our lives differently, according to Paul.

Therefore, the depression we feel from sexual sin is real. And painful. And merciful. If God convicts us of sin, that is a mercy. He is loving us as He convicts us, to draw us to Himself. Conviction of sin means we are not abandoned by God.

Sexual sin is just one example, obviously. There are many other ways in which we might get depressed because of our sin. Like I said, our sin is not the *sole* cause we get depressed. But we must allow for the fact that it might be *a* cause for our depression.

The main point is that we must look at our lives to see if our sin is causing us to feel a certain way. Don't do this alone. That's dangerous. The devil loves to deceive us here. He is the 'accuser of our brothers' (Rev. 12:10). He delights to magnify our sins out of proportion. So, examine yourself but don't do it alone. Get a trusted friend or counselor to come alongside you.

Third, since depression and anxiety are part of life in a fallen world, we do not usually experience these debilitating emotional states through any fault of our own, but simply because we live in a fallen world. This is what makes them so hard. We don't ask to feel down or on edge. These unwelcome and hated intruders oftentimes just appear at our doorstep and barge into our lives, uninvited.

So far, we've focused mainly on depression. What about anxiety? As most of us know from personal experience, anxiety can come in a variety of forms. It might be a panic attack. It might be a low-grade, general uneasiness. Whatever form it takes, anxiety cripples us.

As with depression, so with anxiety. It is a result of the fall. But there is a difference, too. Depression is so hard because it is so often bewildering. It can come out of nowhere. When it comes to anxiety, things get a little simpler. It turns out we have good reason to be anxious.

When Adam and Eve were cast out of the garden, God told them that life would be hard. There would be ground to be subdued, wild beasts to keep away, and the threat of other fallen humans doing bad things to us. In short, life in a fallen world *should* cause us concern. Anxiety is natural, given our circumstances.

So why would God allow us to live in a world that makes us anxious? From the biblical viewpoint, the main thing anxiety does is remind us that we can find peace and calm only in Jesus. In fact, God promises us that we can move away from an anxiety-ridden life, to one of peace and trust. Listen to some of His promises:

> In peace I will both lie down and sleep; for
> you alone, O LORD, make me dwell in safety.
> (Ps. 4:8)

> Great peace have those who love your
> law; nothing can make them stumble.
> (Ps. 119:165)

> You keep him in perfect peace whose mind
> is stayed on you, because he trusts in you.
> (Isa. 26:3)

> Therefore do not be anxious about tomorrow,
> for tomorrow will be anxious for itself.
> Sufficient for the day is its own trouble.
> (Matt. 6:34)

> Do not be anxious about anything, but in
> everything by prayer and supplication with
> thanksgiving let your requests be made
> known to God. And the peace of God, which
> surpasses all understanding, will guard
> your hearts and your minds in Christ Jesus.
> (Phil. 4:6-7)

Did you notice a common theme? God invites us to trust Him in the midst of a world fraught with reasons to make us anxious. David, who was the greatest king of ancient Israel and authored many of the psalms, wrote Psalm 4 when he was in deep distress. Yet, he could talk about sleeping peacefully! Why? Because God was with him.

The prophet Isaiah tells us to stay – fix, concentrate, steel – our minds on God. Jesus tells us we shouldn't be anxious because no one is guaranteed tomorrow. And, if you're a Christian, He says that God will provide for our needs.

The apostle Paul wrote the book of Philippians from a Roman jail cell. He was in horrid conditions. Even there, he could summon his readers against anxiety by laying all their cares on Christ.

This brief overview of the biblical material reveals so much about our struggle with anxiety. We worry, we get anxious because we lose the perspective God offers us in His Word. If we really believed that the God who created the universe was our Father, would we ever be anxious? The answer is obvious.

But life is not so simple, is it? After all, we have seen we have good reason to be anxious. Is God playing games with us? Is He mocking us, telling us not to worry while allowing us to live in a world that gives us every reason to be on edge?

God is not playing games with us. He is recalibrating our hearts. That's what we need when anxiety overwhelms us. We need to re-center ourselves on who God is and what He has promised to do for us (remember what we talked about with God's covenant).

A BIBLICAL PRESCRIPTION FOR DEPRESSION AND ANXIETY

Earlier, we saw the naturalistic evolutionary prescription for these difficulties. But what does the Bible prescribe for anxiety and depression? We don't want to be simplistic or naïve, but we can outline an answer.

First, we must make sure we are Christians. We must examine ourselves, to see if we belong to Jesus (1 Cor. 11:28). The Bible's wisdom on these issues will not help us unless we are in Christ, united to Him in a saving relationship by faith and by faith alone. This is the first and most crucial step.

Second, the Bible tells us that we must believe the promises of God over our present circumstances. One of the best places to turn in Scripture to learn how to do this is Hebrews 11. This chapter contains a long list of biblical characters who triumphed by faith. A common thread running through the stories of each figure is their trust in the bare promises of God.

Think about it. Noah built a gargantuan boat. In. The. Desert (Heb. 11:7). 'Totally crazy,' the folks around him probably said. Consider Abraham. He was promised a child. When he was in his *nineties*. The author of Hebrews put it best when he described Abraham 'as good as dead' (Heb. 11:12).

The list goes on. The point is, these and countless other believers looked beyond what looked so real – their circumstances – and saw the greater reality of God's promises. This is why the author of Hebrews exults, 'These all died in faith, not having received the things promised, but having seen them and greeted them from afar, and having acknowledged that they were strangers and exiles on the earth' (Heb. 11:13). This verse will guide our discussion from here to the end of this chapter.

How do we begin to live like this, when we struggle with anxiety and depression? The same way these ancient saints did. The author of Hebrews tells us how.

He gets specific. He puts legs on the concept of faith. According to the author of Hebrews, faith means *seeing* and *receiving* the reality of what is promised, even when we don't possess it. (Heb. 11:1)

Let's make this practical. When we get anxious or depressed, we are dealing with *mental* health problems. The battle is for our minds. Therefore, we must train our minds to *see* the unseen and *receive* that which we do not have. We do this by daily practices like reading the Bible, meditating on it, and speaking truth to ourselves.

Psychologists have shown that daily habits can help us tremendously with our mental health problems. Habits such as getting enough sleep, exercising regularly, and eating a proper diet are just a few examples. By far, the most important daily habit for our mental health is immersing ourselves in God's Word.

God's promises in His Word allow us to receive as real what we only see by faith. 'We walk by faith, not by sight' in this life (2 Cor. 5:7). As we train our minds, a new narrative begins to unfold. We begin to see the world as it really is – from God's point of view.

THE DOCTOR'S PRESCRIPTION

Dr. Martyn Lloyd-Jones, possibly the greatest preacher of the last century, highlights the importance of training our minds. Prior to being a minister, he was one of the leading physicians in England. In fact, fresh out of medical school he was the assistant to the chief physician of the king of England. He walked away from this promising career to begin ministering God's Word to some of the poorest people in his native Wales. From there, he was called to Westminster Chapel in London, which sits just across the street from Buckingham Palace. His renowned career in medicine, pulpit acumen, and personal devotion earned the respect of all who knew him. To show that respect, they began calling Lloyd-Jones simply, 'The Doctor.'

He saw his church through the terrors of the *blitzkrieg* and *Luftwaffe* raids in World War II. His ministry exercised global influence. I mention this background so you know that Lloyd-Jones was not preaching or writing as a disinterested observer in our mental health difficulties. Far from it. He lived in the middle of one of the greatest wars in world history. For over a year, he faced the prospect of death by a *Luftwaffe* bombing. If anyone should have been anxious, it was the citizens of London during this time.

After the war ended, Lloyd-Jones was burdened by the tremendous psychological toll it had taken on his congregation and nation. So he preached a series of sermons that became a bestselling book, *Spiritual Depression: Its Causes and Cures*. It remains a classic to this day for the insights it provides into anxiety and depression.

In the first chapter of that book, he asks this revealing question. 'Have you ever realized that most of the unhappiness in your life is due to the fact that you are listening to yourself instead of talking to yourself?'[6]

Lloyd-Jones has put his finger on maybe the central issue for our mental health. How we talk to ourselves is one of our main problems, not only when we face

---

6. D. Martyn Lloyd-Jones, *Spiritual Depression: Its Causes and Cures* (London: Marshall Pickering, 1998), p. 20.

depression and anxiety, but in day-to-day life. Therefore, getting control of our inner monologue is key.

Let's return to what the author of Hebrews told us above. He urges us, 'Look at these great believers of the past. What did they have in common? They *spoke* the promises of God to themselves, even as they *listened* to the promises.'

Again, I'm not saying our depression or anxiety disappears overnight if we just do this one simple step. I am saying that unless we replace our inner self-talk with God's Word, we are missing out on one of His primary means to ease our depression and anxiety.

Identity, Depression, and Anxiety

Finally, we must remember our identity. We are 'strangers and exiles,' if we are Christians. In other words, we are homeless even if we live in a mansion. We are strangers even if we are natural-born citizens of the country where we live, surrounded by friends.

The identity piece of this puzzle is so important to our mental health. It's closely related to how we talk to ourselves. What we say to ourselves reveals what we believe about ourselves. If we have a constant inner voice of shame, our identity becomes 'Not good enough.' If our inner voice is anxiety, our identity becomes 'Won't be provided for.' If our inner voice is depression, our identity becomes, 'Hopeless.'

The author of Hebrews gives us fresh hope by offering us new categories. He tells us that we must remember our true identity – 'Not of this world.' We will never feel fully at home in this life if we are Christians. Even our best moments will be tainted by sin. Because of the fall, we were never meant to be satisfied fully in this life. Why? Because God has placed in us a 'holy discontent' for Himself. Let me explain.

Abraham was a wealthy man. So was Noah. Despite their wealth and comfort, the Bible tells us that God enabled them to live for the life to come. In other words, because they believed God's promises to them and because all of God's promises find their fulfillment in Jesus, they were 'ancient Christians.'

Just like them, we are to live for an unseen, better world, while living in this world. This is not escapism. This is not pie-in-the-sky thinking. This is reality, according to God. The real world, says the author of Hebrews, is not what we see, but what is unseen and grasped by faith. Once again, perspective makes all the difference.

The language of 'strangers and exiles' – identity language – is not a stray thought in God's Word. The Bible is filled with identity language. Christians are 'beloved children' (Eph. 5:1), 'sons of God' (Rom. 8:14), and 'chosen' (Col. 3:12). And so much more. The bottom line is that until we find our identity in what God says about us, we will never understand who we really are.

So, living by faith means living out our identity as strangers and exiles. Once we begin to knead this identity into our souls, our grip loosens on the things of this world. That will help our anxiety. Understanding our identity as deeply loved children of God will also begin to shine a light into our darkest moments of depression.

Where do you find your identity? Is it in your possessions? Your physical strength? Your artistic skill? Your brilliant mind? The simple test to discern where we are looking to find our identity is this. What do you look to for meaning, encouragement, and security? If it's anything other than God, we will experience a case of 'mistaken identity.'

The good news is that Jesus gives us back our true identity. There are no fake IDs in heaven! He rescues us from all of our false trusts, false identities, and mistaken allegiances. We must anchor ourselves in what God says about us, not what the world around or the voices within tell us.

WE HAVE NOTHING TO FEAR BUT FEAR ITSELF

Finally, let's talk about fear. In his speech declaring war on Japan in December of 1941, President Franklin D. Roosevelt said the immortal words, 'We have nothing to fear but fear itself.' Inspiring, to be sure. But is it true? That depends on what we mean by fear.

In one sense, fear is good. Fear is God-given. We've all heard of the 'fight or flight' instinct. God gave us fear, in the form of flight, to preserve our lives. If a lion is running at us, God designed our bodies to increase adrenaline flow, heart rate, and other triggers in our biological systems to enable us to flee for our lives. That kind of fear is good.

But there is a wrong kind of fear. It takes many forms. It could be an inordinate fear of something in creation, what we typically call a *phobia*. This kind of fear is disproportionate to the object that is feared. For instance, *arachnophobia* is an unhealthy fear of spiders. To be sure, a phobia like this is not necessarily sinful. It's just disjointed.

We all have our phobias. Most of the time, we just get on with our lives and avoid those things that cause us to have unbalanced fear. That's one kind of wrong fear.

In reality, at the heart of any kind of *wrong* fear is a lack of the *right* kind of fear. The Bible tells us that a distinguishing mark of someone who knows God is that this person fears God. The wisest man besides Jesus who ever lived, King Solomon of ancient Israel, said, 'Fear God and keep his commandments, for this is the whole duty of man' (Eccles. 12:13). The right kind of fear – the fear we all need – is the fear of God.

Fearing God is not the same thing as a phobia kind of fear. It is totally different. Many authors have captured what it means to fear God by defining it as 'reverential awe.' That's a good definition of what it means to fear God. This kind of fear produces love, not repulsion. When you're afraid of spiders, you're never going to love them. You'll be revolted by them.

However, I'm sure there are people in your life that you hold in awe. Maybe it's a parent, friend, or sibling. That person inspires respect in you, even reverence. You hold them in the highest esteem. There are traits and characteristics about that person that have captivated you. So, in this sense, you 'fear' them. And this fear does not drive you away from them; it draws you to them.

As I write, my father is eighty-six. He is certainly not a perfect man. But, to this day, I hold him in deep respect. He was an actor and taught theater, so he has a booming voice. When my brothers and I were growing up, we knew we were in trouble when my dad said our full names with that big, deep voice. We were, to say the least, alarmed when our names were called in that tone!

But we always knew he loved us. So I don't fear my dad, in the wrong sense. I fear him because I respect him and know he loves me.

In a far greater sense, this is how the fear of God should function in our lives. It should draw us in, even as it makes us fall on our faces in awe. This kind of fear is healthy. In fact, the fear of God is the only kind of fear that will free us from all other fears.

Listen to how Jesus put it. 'Do not fear those who kill the body but cannot kill the soul. Rather fear him who can destroy both soul and body in hell' (Matt. 10:28). Notice the contrasts. Fearing 'those' versus fearing 'him.' Body and soul. This life versus the life to come. Jesus is deliberate here, framing the issue in blunt terms. He wants to provide comfort for His disciples facing persecution. So this *command* comes as a *comfort*. But it is stark and unrelenting and honest. And so helpful.

How is this command helpful? Consider how uneasy most of us (the vast majority of us, I would venture) are at the prospect of our own deaths. We do all we can to preserve our lives. That's a good thing. God wants us to take the necessary steps to prolong our lives. We're not to have a death-wish.

Jesus, however, tells us that following Him will cost us our lives. He doesn't mean that all His followers will die *physically* in His service. He means that we have to surrender everything to Him. And that might mean losing our physical lives because the world hates Him and kills Christians for being Christians.

This is why He says, 'Don't fear what people can do to you. After all, once they kill you, that's all they can do to you.' He's not minimizing how terrible it would be to lose our lives. Instead, He's giving us the right perspective on the worth of our lives and the reality of our approaching death. In a nutshell, Jesus is reminding us that this life and death are both temporary. One day, our bodies will be raised and death will be no more (Rev. 21:4). Jesus gives us perspective, which helps us deal with our fears.

DEALING WITH FEAR

Fearing God is not a popular concept today. I'm old enough to remember my grandparents describing others as 'God-fearing people.' That was a common phrase for their generation. Today, however, many Christians shy away from mentioning the fear of God.

However, we need to rediscover what Jesus offers us in these verses. We must cultivate a healthy fear of God in our lives if we are to have any hope of overcoming our fears. How do we do that?

First, *we get to know God as He really is*. Not what we want Him to be. Not what the culture around us imagines Him to be, but who the Bible says He is. One of the defining characteristics of the biblical God is that He is holy. He is 'other.' He is beautiful, awe-inspiring, majestic, praiseworthy, blameless, sinless, undefiled, awesome, and countless other adjectives that can be summed up with the word *holy*.

God's absolute holiness means that He cannot tolerate sin. The prophet Habakkuk cries out, 'You who are of purer eyes than to see evil and cannot look at wrong' (Hab. 1:13). God's holiness is not just sacred; it's terrifying. For, sinful creatures cannot stand before a holy God.

This observation leads to our second point: *we accept the Bible's diagnosis of who we really are*. We are sinners. We have nothing to boast about. We have nothing to commend us to this holy God. We are lost, helpless, and hopeless apart from His love and grace to us in Jesus by the Holy Spirit. Until we see ourselves as we really are, we will never see God for who He really is.

Unless and until we see God and ourselves truly, we will never be amazed by His grace. Instead of 'Amazing Grace,' we'll sing something like, 'Ordinary grace, how bland the sound, that saved a semi-good, definitely not a wretch, person like me.' In order for grace to be amazing, an awareness of God's holiness and our sinfulness must not simply be theological abstractions, but intimate realities in our lives.

The good news is that God's grace really is amazing. It is unique. Other religions have some concept of a holy

God or gods. None of them teach that the holiness God requires is the holiness He provides for unholy people like us, through the life, death, and resurrection of Jesus. What God's holiness requires, His amazing grace provides for us in Jesus. Isn't that wonderful?

Finally, if we want to begin to overcome fear, we *must live with the perspective of eternity.* That's the point of Jesus' admonition to His fretful little band of disciples we examined above. He knows they will be afraid of torture and persecution and death. So He gives them perspective.

We may never face such things. But we all need perspective because everything around us puts life out of proportion. A lot of our fear stems from this disproportion. We worry about an issue or problem in our lives and it grows bigger and bigger. We lose perspective and fear takes over. The cycle repeats itself.

There is a spiritual economics lesson here. To the degree and proportion our improper fears grow, to that same degree and proportion our fear of God diminishes. Mercifully, God's grace is not a zero-sum economic theory. In other words, there is always more of God's grace for our misplaced fears. More good news!

Jesus offers us such a merciful rescue here. He gently brings us back to the real world – His world. He reminds us that all of our fear should be God-sized. In other words, the vantage point you choose will determine the size of your fear.

In sum, we will only bring our fears down to size if we upsize, as it were, our fear of God. Today, why not stop and write down what you fear the most? Now, next to that fear, write these two, simple words, 'But God.' For example, 'I am afraid that I will die alone.' 'But God has promised me he will be with me' (Ps. 23:4). Or, 'I am afraid of heights.' 'But God will protect me' (Ps. 91:11-12). Those two words, repeated so often in Scripture, help us reprioritize our fears and thereby recalibrate our lives.

In short, the Bible offers us a much different take on depression, anxiety, and fear. Not only is the biblical viewpoint different, it is true and it works. God did not create us to live a life of fear, but freedom (John 8:32). When we begin to meditate on God's holiness, our sinfulness, and His provision for all our fears, we will learn to fear – and love – God, which will help us with every fear we face in this life.

CONCLUSION

I mentioned in the introduction that I grew up going to the beaches of North and South Carolina with my family. I remember vividly one of those trips. My parents had given me a new boogie board which is a kind of mini-surfboard. I was probably ten or eleven years old. I grabbed it and crashed into the surf, eager to see if I could ride one of the waves to bring me back to shore.

What I didn't realize is that I jumped straight into a rip current. The roar of the ocean muted my parents' warning cries as I ran into the foaming sea. I remember being taken under and finding myself unable to get above water. I began to panic and struggle, the two responses one should not have in these situations. I was only making things worse! I needed a rescue.

Suddenly, two strong arms yanked me from underneath the water and threw me out of the rip current. My older brother had seen me jump into the current and came running after me. The whole incident happened in just a few seconds, but, for the rest of our vacation, I looked long and hard at the currents before I went on another boogie-board adventure. I learned how dangerous a day at the beach could be.

The author of Hebrews tells us that Jesus is our spiritual older brother (Heb. 2:11-12). Like my brother did for me, a good older brother rescues us when we're helpless. Whether we're overcome by depression, anxiety, or fear, Jesus wants to rescue us. Knowing Jesus is our older brother makes His words to us all the more powerful. 'Let not your hearts be troubled. Believe in God; believe also in me … I go and prepare a place for you' (John 14:1-3). Only an older brother who is God in the flesh can say to us, 'Let not your hearts be troubled' and have the ability to keep that promise. When you're sinking, the everlasting arms of Jesus will rescue you.

If you are not a Christian, I recognize that a lot of what we have covered so far may be startling, but hopefully intriguing! Let me encourage you to keep reading. In the last chapter, I have some recommendations for how you might proceed if you're curious about what it means to become a Christian.

4

What Does the Bible Say About Illness, Disability, and Death?

It's winter as I write this, which means at least half the people I know are sick. If they have small children (or if you have or have had them), you know they bring home every ailment under the sun from school. So they won't be well for months. Winter makes me sick of being sick.

Illness and disease have plagued mankind since time immemorial. But, in the last one hundred years, we have made astonishing progress in battling all kinds of diseases. I know we're all thankful for modern medicine.

Still, humankind is plagued by plagues. As we saw in the last chapter, the biblical explanation for things like illness and death is the fall of mankind into sin. Adam's sin had far-reaching and catastrophic penalties. Death is the culmination of all illnesses; it is the ultimate penalty for Adam's sin.

Ever since the fateful day in the Garden of Eden, humans have sought to conquer death and illness. Yuval Noah Harari, bestselling author and outspoken transhumanist (the belief that the human race will evolve beyond our current limitations through technological advances), insists that we are on the verge of achieving this goal. With an optimism that can only be described as religious, he writes, 'Most people rarely think about it, but in the last few decades we have managed to rein in famine, plague, and war … we don't need to pray to any god or saint to rescue us from them. We know quite well what needs to be done in order to prevent famine, plague and war – and we usually succeed in doing it.'[1]

Harari published his book in 2017. Since that time, a worldwide pandemic, wars in Ukraine and Israel, and widespread social unrest, have ravaged the planet. As a result, the reader can be forgiven if he does not share quite the same confidence Harari prophesies. True, there is a lot of data that demonstrates humanity is doing much better in many areas. But sickness, death, and disability show no signs of going away anytime soon.

The first two all of us will face. The last one, disability, only some of us will experience. But all three are painful,

---

1. Yuval Noah Harari, *Homo Deus: A Brief History of Tomorrow* (New York: Harper Perennial, 2017), pp. 1-2.

daily realities of life. What is God doing in our lives when we face these things? Does He care? These are some of the questions we will try to answer in this chapter.

ILLNESS

Let's start with the first affliction mentioned above, illness. From a biblical standpoint, when God made the world, sickness was not present. And even if you get well, eventually all of us will die. Sickness is a result of the fall and so is death. As a result, we cannot escape illness or death on this side of eternity.

Think about it like this. Every healing from illness we experience in this life is *temporary*. None of us are ever healed completely. Our bodies break down continually and will succumb at last to death.

'Great,' you say to yourself. 'More good news in this chapter.' Stay with me! As I said at the outset, I believe the Bible offers us so much hope when faced with the bleak prospect of a life beset with sickness ending in death.

If our healing is only temporary, so also are our sicknesses. For most of us, when we speak about 'getting sick,' we mean something temporary. Thanks to the medical advances mentioned above, sickness has become an inconvenience rather than a way of life.

Of course, this has not always been the case. The vast majority of people who have walked this earth stayed unwell throughout their lives. One writer illustrates this severe reality using John Calvin's story as an example. Note that what he says would easily apply to the previous centuries and millennia that came before Calvin's time. 'Life was harsh, even brutal, in the sixteenth century. There was no sewer system or piped water supply … or antibiotics or penicillin or aspirin or surgery … Calvin, like many others in his day, suffered from "almost continuous ill-health."'[2] Read those last phrases again. 'Like many others.' 'Continuous ill-health.' The fact that less than five hundred years later, I could write most of us do *not* suffer from continuous ill health is astonishing.

So I agree, in part, with Harari. As I said, the data show that we are getting healthier. And while most of the sickness we experience is, in fact, temporary, we know all too well that chronic illnesses affect millions of people. Distressing realities like cancer, autoimmune diseases, and inexplicable constant pain are daily realities for many people in this life.

Both temporary and chronic sickness can serve as powerful arguments against the existence of a kind, merciful God. Both challenge us to ask hard questions. But both can also teach us more about God than we imagined.

---

2. John Piper, *The Legacy of Sovereign Joy: God's Triumphant Grace in the Lives of Augustine, Luther, and Calvin* (Wheaton, IL: Crossway Books, 2000), p. 33.

JESUS AND SICKNESS

If you're skeptical about the Bible's veracity, let me ask your patience as we walk through an account from one of the Gospels. It will help us make sense of God's relationship to sickness.

One of the best proofs of the Bible's truthfulness is how ordinary it is. By that I mean the people we meet in its pages are folks we can relate to. In the fifth chapter of the Gospel of Mark (the second book in the New Testament), we meet one of these types, a man named Jairus. He was a lay ruler of the synagogue. To set the context, the synagogue was the epicenter of Jewish life. So Jairus would have been seen by the people of that time as a combination of a therapist, legal advisor, and spiritual guide.

He comes to Jesus in great distress. Even approaching Jesus was a risky move on Jairus's part. No doubt he had heard about this traveling preacher and rabbi from Nazareth. He knew the religious authorities in Jerusalem – his higher-ups – did not approve of Jesus.

No matter. His 'little daughter is at the point of death' (v. 23). When your child is sick and dying, the boss's opinion is the last thing on your mind. All Jairus knew was that everyone was talking about the miracles Jesus worked throughout the region. So, he 'implored Him earnestly' (v. 23). This is the desperate cry of parental love. Jesus goes with Jairus to help him.

Here's where the story gets really interesting. As Jesus is walking with Jairus – a panicked, grieving father – crowds press in. All are clamoring for Jesus' attention. Remember this is first-century Israel. No one had bathed in days, maybe months. It's loud and smelly.

Out of this seething, thronging mass steps a woman. We are told she 'had had a discharge of blood for twelve years' and 'suffered much under many physicians' (Mark 5:25-26). Some more cultural background is necessary for us to grasp fully what happens next.

To begin, women in first-century Israel did not just come up and touch a rabbi, like this woman would do. That would be a social *faux pas* on the level of barging into a classroom at Harvard and sitting on the professor's lap. She would have been taught her whole life about the respect accorded to rabbis, meaning that one did not simply walk up to them and try to touch them. But when we're desperate, social graces fall away quickly.

Second, since this woman had an issue of blood for well over a decade, she would have been ceremonially unclean for that entire time, as detailed in the book of Leviticus (Lev. 15:19-25). What did it mean to be 'ceremonially unclean'? Without getting lost in the details, God gave His Old Testament people different kinds of laws. Some of them pertained to the ways that the Israelites were to worship (the 'ceremonies' they were to follow, hence *ceremonial* law). The main purpose of these laws was, first and foremost, to teach them about the coming Messiah, Jesus. But they also taught them about God's holiness – His separateness from the world and sin.

Thus, when God gave this law, He was not being harsh or sexist. He was teaching His people about His holiness. That's why, in the same chapter in Leviticus, He prescribes how someone like this woman could be made ceremonially *clean* and return to the normal life of worship in the Israelite community.

Now, with that background in mind, let's make this woman more than just a character in the story. To understand her, we need to meet her on her terms. She was Jewish. Her whole life revolved around her religion. This kind of religious lifestyle is foreign to many of us in the West, but it was the norm in this culture.

Since her life centered around going to the synagogue and the temple (the custom was once a year for temple worship) and since she had an issue of blood for twelve years which made her ceremonially unclean, this means she was cut off from all community. Anyone who came near her would have been defiled simply by contact with her. Therefore, everyone stayed away.

Can you imagine being friendless and isolated for twelve *years*? I know I can't. Day in, day out, the same thing. The numbing monotony of loneliness was the only song this woman's heart had known for a long time.

As if that wasn't bad enough, she is now poor. The text tells us she spent 'all that she had' on doctors (v. 26). Maybe you can relate. Maybe you experience chronic illness and now you are facing financial difficulties. We have celebrated the triumphs of modern medicine, but we all know that it comes with a steep price. Medical care was no different in the ancient world. It was expensive. Worse, it usually didn't work, as was the case with this woman.

In a word, she has everything going against her. She's a woman, friendless, and broke. She's at the bottom of the social and religious structure of that time.

You can bet she wondered, 'Where are You, God? Why are You letting me suffer like this? And all by myself? All of my people have learned for centuries that You are merciful. This doesn't feel like mercy.' Don't we ask the same questions when we are sick for a long time?

Then Jesus arrives on the scene and suddenly that monotony is broken. For the first time, she has hope because she has heard about 'Jesus of Nazareth, the miracle worker.' She casts aside all the social and religious norms of her time and rushes to find Jesus when she hears that He is nearby.

Her faith is just amazing. The Bible tells us she said to herself, 'If I touch even the hem of his garments, I will be made well.' No doubts. No hesitation. She doesn't even need to speak to or meet Jesus! She has complete, utter trust in the ability of this man she does not know. So she does what she planned. She touches Him and immediately she is healed.

Now, again, return to the scene. It was already chaotic – people crowding in on Jesus, Jairus urging Him along, and then this woman straining her way through this crowd, grasping for just a bit of Jesus' clothing. Mark records that Jesus perceived that power 'had gone out from him' (v. 30) after she touched Him. That is beautiful. Jesus is not a talisman, or a statue. This woman didn't come to a magic shrine that was indifferent to her troubles. With maybe hundreds of people touching Him, He still knows that a *certain person* has touched Him.

Things get even more frenzied from here. He stops and asks who touched Him. His disciples react the way many of us would – they're incredulous. 'Look at the crowd!' they say. 'What do you mean who touched You? The answer is, literally *everyone*!' They didn't realize yet that Jesus is a *personal* Savior who knew *everything* about *everyone* who touched Him, but this woman had touched Him *in faith*.

Return to the scene. She has been found out. She falls at His feet, expecting the worst – she came with 'fear and trembling' (v. 33). Note that she has already been healed. A new life had been opened for her at once. But she would have to face the consequences of her actions. Or so she thought.

Most rabbis would have been repulsed by her and then enraged that she had defiled them by her touch. They would have cast her away. Not Jesus.

He wasn't and isn't like other religious teachers. I love how He responds to her. 'Daughter,' He calls her. Remember He is going to see Jairus's daughter, but another daughter needed His help first. He doesn't rebuke her. He doesn't hurry on His way. He speaks tenderly to her and gives her all the assurance she needs. 'Your faith has made you well; go in peace and be healed of your disease' (v. 34).

If she's already healed, why does He say, 'Be healed'? Because He knew that everyone around was watching. In His love and kindness, He uses His position as a respected teacher to inform the crowd that this woman is now clean. She can return to community, worship, socializing – *life*. Jesus is not only a powerful Savior, but a considerate one. He takes care of people holistically. This woman woke up that morning living in grayscale and went to sleep that night with the promise of the colored landscape of hope.

What Jesus' Response Teaches Us About Sickness

What does this story teach us about our own illness and how Jesus responds to us when we're sick? We could spend chapter after chapter answering that question, but let's limit ourselves to a few observations.

First, like this woman, we must go to Jesus when we're sick. Have you ever tried that? Don't mistake me. Faith does not mean that we don't use the means God has given us to heal our bodies, like medicine and doctors. But God can still heal where doctors can't.

You may be really skeptical about this. You might say, 'Seriously? How can we still believe in miraculous healings?' Let's ask a different question. Why *wouldn't* we believe in miracles?

Someone might argue, 'Because science has shown us that there are natural laws that simply cannot be violated. Miracles are a violation of natural law and therefore do not happen.' Is that a good argument against miracles in general and miraculous healings in particular?

I don't think so. Science cannot prove that nature is uniform, which is the crucial presupposition that underwrites the whole concept of 'natural laws' in the first premise of the argument above. This premise simply begs the question – it assumes what the argument is supposed to prove.

In addition, thinking of miracles as 'violations of natural law' also begs the question. It assumes the biblical account isn't true without meeting it on its own terms. The Bible never describes the universe as a closed system, in which God is not involved. Again, one must *assume* that view of the universe. But where's the proof of *that* assumption?

Consider this fact also. Whenever Jesus performs a miracle, the Gospel authors record it somewhat indifferently – as if to say, 'No big deal. It's Jesus. *Of course* He does stuff like this. Now focus on *Him*, not the miracle.'

Again, this kind of attitude on the part of the biblical writers towards miracles should reinforce a conviction of the Bible's truthfulness. If we were going to make up a religion, we would want everyone to know about the miracles our invented god was performing. We would make a huge fuss over them. The Bible does just the opposite. If you read the Gospels, Jesus almost goes out of His way to downplay His miracles.

So, it's safe to conclude that Jesus can still heal us today. For example, I met a woman a few years ago who came to faith in Jesus (she was an avowed and very well-educated atheist) when her husband was cured of stage-four brain cancer after a prayer meeting. I could multiply stories like these that I've witnessed first-hand in the ministry.

On the other hand, I could also recount the many deathbeds I've sat beside where earnest Christians prayed fervently for healing that did not come – at least not in the way they asked for it. As I mentioned before, what always amazes and encourages me is that these people who did not get the healing they asked for continued in their faith. Why? Because they believed and understood our bedrock truth #1 – God is sovereign. They knew that God is sovereign over our sickness *and* our healing.

Here's where things get hard for us. Questions like, 'Why does Jesus heal some and not others?' bombard us. Or we might ask, 'Why wouldn't Jesus heal everyone?' I don't have all the answers, of course.

Here's what I *do* know. I do know Jesus is good, kind, and merciful. I do know He can choose to heal. Where we struggle, I think, is that Jesus seems, well, *arbitrary* when it comes to healing. He's not.

How do we know He's not arbitrary? If we believe that Jesus is God (as the Bible teaches over and over), then He is sovereign. This means He has a reason for everything He does, even if we don't know all those reasons. In fact, He never guaranteed that we would have that kind of knowledge.

Finally, when we pray for healing and we aren't healed in the way we ask, I can hear someone protesting (and have heard this!), 'See! Prayer doesn't work.'

Once again, we must engage with God on His terms. In other words, what if we're wrong about the terms of prayer? A lot of people tend to think of prayer as guesswork or a shot in the dark, a kind of last resort. But the Bible tells us that, like Jairus and the woman we met, when we pray, we must pray with faith and trust God with the results. So prayer is not a magical incantation or a long shot. It is confident trust that God knows best what we need, even if we don't understand why He answers the way He does.

Sickness, like other forms of suffering, reveals our deepest assumptions about who God is. Most of the arguments we raise against God's healing activity are based on mistaken assumptions about the nature of God and the nature of faith. If we are willing to question those assumptions, we can open ourselves up to experience the same kind of miraculous intervention this woman witnessed – if God chooses.

JESUS AND DEATH

This scene from Mark 5 also teaches us how Jesus helps us cope with death. We all hate the subject of death, but the Bible does not shy away from it. As I was thinking about our antipathy towards death, I was reminded of an experience from my graduate school days.

I had a professor from Norway, who was a brilliant philosopher with a compassionate heart. We were studying the work of Martin Heidegger, the existentialist philosopher of the last century, who grappled with death throughout his illustrious career. As we were working through some of his writings, she made an offhand observation in class one day that stuck with me. She said, 'You Americans do not handle death well. I don't understand all the lipstick and makeup on a corpse.' She was not a Christian, but she understood the reality of death far better than most Christians. Like Heidegger, she knew that you couldn't dress up death and make it pretty. Death is ugly.

Numerous cultural observers have noted that death seems to be the last taboo subject in Western life. You can go to a social gathering and hear conversations about graphic sexual escapades and most people won't feel awkward. You can mention any number of topics that were long considered 'out of bounds' for discussion in polite company and see folks nod in agreement.

Start talking about death and see what happens. Eyes dart around the room, people suddenly find themselves drawn to the *hors d'oeuvres*, and nervous whispers begin.

Isn't this ironic? It's not like death is something rare or exotic. Every one of us will die. We all know the old adage – 'The only two certainties in life are death and taxes.' All of us face it. All of us will experience it. Yet we can't stand even saying the word – we use euphemisms with ease when speaking of death. We are a strange lot.

In reality, I think the reason we shrink away from ever thinking about, let alone discussing, death is that we are hardwired by God to know that it is unnatural. Death is not part of the 'circle of life,' as the movie *The Lion King* enshrined in our cultural memory. As we have seen, death is a result of Adam's sin. It is unnatural, foreign, and terrible.

According to the Bible, we were never meant to go to funerals. We were never meant to shovel dirt over the casket of someone we love. This is why the apostle Paul could say that death was 'the last enemy' (1 Cor. 15:26).

Let's go back to Mark 5. After healing one daughter, Jesus finally arrives at Jairus's house. But He is stopped by the synagogue ruler's servants. You can hear their despondency. 'Your daughter is dead. Why trouble the Teacher any further?' (v. 35). Jairus's heart probably sank. As the waves of grief began to overwhelm him at this news, he hears another voice. Jesus says, 'Do not fear, only believe' (v. 36). The Savior has not forgotten him.

What happens next is just as breathtaking – and revealing – as what Jesus did with the woman He healed a few moments earlier. He arrives at Jairus's house and, as was the custom, professional mourners were already on the scene. In this culture, these people were paid to weep, wail, and lament. This was also a society in which large families were the rule, not the exception. So there's a lot of people, a lot of noise, and not a lot of hope.

Jesus says to them, in effect, 'What's all the fuss about? She's sleeping. I am going to wake her.' The crowd 'laughed at him' (v. 40). The word here in Greek suggests a kind of scornful laughing. We all know its sound – the kind of laugh that has no joy but only cynicism. The kind of laugh that says, 'I used to laugh for delight. Now I laugh to deride.'

Jesus puts them and their scorn out of the house. In other words, He de-escalates the situation. He takes Jairus and his wife, along with His disciples, and comes into the room where the girl's body is lying. Throughout this whole scene, we're not told what Jairus said. But I have to believe, as a father myself, that he was hanging on every word from Jesus. After all, he had just witnessed the healing of this woman.

Consider this also: Jairus probably *knew* the woman with the issue of blood. He probably had to see her every day and make sure he avoided contact with her so he could perform his duties at the synagogue. He had to make a living by avoiding her dying life. But now she is whole. This is running through his mind – 'If He did it for her, then He can help my daughter.' He finds himself at the intersection of grief, wonder, worship, and terror.

Jesus leans over the bed. If we were onlookers, maybe the only sounds we would have heard were the hushed sobs of Jairus and his wife. The Lord takes their daughter by the hand and speaks to her in Aramaic, which was the language spoken by Jews at this time. He says, 'Talitha, cumi,' which means 'Little girl, I say to you, arise' (v. 41).

Picture the look on Jairus's face when his daughter sat up! Open-mouthed astonishment. Too much to take in. Jesus knows this will be the parents' reaction, so He continues to care for this little girl. He tells them to give her something to eat. He truly is a powerful and caring Savior.

HOW JESUS HELPS US THINK ABOUT DEATH

There's so much we can learn about death from Jesus' actions in this marvelous account.

First, *Jesus rules over death*. He raises this poor girl with a few words. His power is unlimited! In fact, her resurrection is a 'preview of coming attractions' – the One who raises her with a word will Himself be raised without a word.

Many people today believe that death is the end of everything. You live, you die – that's it. Again, no one can live out this answer consistently. Why? Because if life is *ultimately* meaningless and death is final, then any meaning we find in the here and now is an illusion – a blind leap of faith.

I remember when the wave of the 'New Atheists' came crashing upon the cultural shoreline. One of their favorite terms to deride believers was 'faith heads.' I found this term ironic since the new atheists proclaimed that nature is all there is. Again, on this view, when we die, that's the end of us.

They then went on to argue that, despite this seemingly hopeless outlook, we could still find meaning. This is why I thought their name-calling was ironic. It seemed to me that the real 'faith heads' were those who could believe something as absurd as the reality of temporary meaning when there is no ultimate meaning. You cannot have the former without the latter.

Back to Jesus' resuscitation of Jairus's daughter. This episode also teaches us that *Jesus cares for us when we face death*. He is the ultimate Good Shepherd foreshadowed by Psalm 23 – when we walk through the valley of the shadow of death, He is with us, guiding us by His rod and staff (Ps. 23:4).

We need to be honest with ourselves here. We can put on a brave face when we talk about death, especially if we're young and healthy. We may boast that we aren't afraid of death. But nothing in our lives can prepare us for actually dying. I think we're all a lot more afraid of this experience than we let on.

So how can we have real hope when we face death? Jesus' resurrection of this little girl was a signpost pointing to His own resurrection. Because He is alive, we can have real hope.

Maybe you struggle to believe in the resurrection of Jesus. Certainly, you're not alone. The claim that Jesus rose from the dead has been attacked since the moment He stepped out of the empty tomb. The problem for the critics and skeptics of Jesus' resurrection is that, try as they might, they can't disprove it. There's too much evidence and it is too overwhelming to ignore.[3]

At a deeper level, though, the problem has never been the *evidence* for Jesus' resurrection. The issue has always been the *worldview* we use to interpret that evidence. In his delightful book *Miracles*, C. S. Lewis, the celebrated author and Christian apologist of the last century, gets to the heart of the problem we have with believing miracles. He writes, 'The question whether miracles occur can never be answered by experience ... what we learn from experience depends on the kind of philosophy we bring to experience.'[4]

So the problem is not the evidence for the resurrection of Jesus. We'll misread the evidence unless we are willing to question the philosophy of experience, to use Lewis's terms, that we bring to the evidence.

Therefore, if we struggle to believe that Jesus is alive, we can study the evidence for His resurrection.

---

3.   For a summary of arguments for the indisputable proof of Jesus' resurrection, see Gary R. Habermas, *Risen Indeed: A Historical Investigation into the Resurrection of* Jesus (Bellingham, WA: Lexham Academic, 2021).

4.   C. S. Lewis, *Miracles* (New York: Harper One, 2001), pp. 1-2.

We can weigh it and discuss it, but until we are willing to surrender our worldview and have Jesus replace it with a worldview based on His Word, we will never believe in the resurrection.

If you're not a Christian, what has your current worldview provided for you that you think will help you as you face disease, disability, and death? More importantly, is your worldview *true*? Can it stand up to scrutiny? Death is the most serious event of our lives so we would do well to be sure we understand it and what happens after it. We should not shy away from asking our worldview some hard questions. If you're willing to do this, I think you'll find that only Christianity can stand up to the difficult questions you ask.

At the core of the Christian worldview is the fact that Jesus is alive. Coupled with this fact is His offer that we can be alive with Him, spiritually in this life and, one day, spiritually and physically in a resurrection body. Knowing this changes everything, both in this life and in the life to come!

Because of the resurrection of Jesus, we can begin to face the reality of death with confidence. We don't have to settle for a hopeless worldview of nihilism. He offers us a better way to deal with death because He is the only one who has ever defeated death.

THE BIBLE AND DISABILITIES

Finally, we come to the last ailment we will cover in this chapter, disability. You may have been born with a disability or you may have lived some of your life without any disabilities, only to find yourself with one now. Whatever your circumstances, living with a disability makes it very, very hard to believe in the goodness of God.

I learned this lesson long before I became a Christian. When I was in college, I was in a fraternity. I recognize that most people's impression of fraternities and sororities is a crowd of sex-crazed, drunken revelers. There are plenty of people in fraternities and sororities matching that description. Certainly, those kinds of things happened in my fraternity.

Still, every fraternity has a philanthropy they support. My fraternity started its own philanthropy to serve people with disabilities. Our work with people with disabilities brought out the best of my fraternity brothers.

Each summer, members from all over the country staged two separate bicycle treks, one across the US and one covering the state of Florida. Three times I cycled about 1,100 miles, zigzagging up the state of Florida. The structure was simple: our team would ride about one hundred miles a day and stay in local towns, serving people with disabilities. They were transformative experiences for me. They helped me see that there was a lot more to life than drinking, partying, and socializing.

Most importantly, after spending so much time with people with disabilities, I realized how much I could learn from them. They did not let their disabilities define them. Most of them were resilient, joyful people. It was humbling to be around them.

Looking back, I now know that a lot of the people I met were Christians. I even remember one of them talking to me about Jesus! How could they love Jesus when they were suffering from various disabilities? A story from the Bible will once again help us answer this question.

JESUS AND THE MAN BORN BLIND

This time, we'll go to the Gospel according to John, chapter 9. Jesus' disciples ask Him a question about a blind man they just passed near the temple complex.

Intriguingly, their question reveals a fairly modern attitude towards suffering in general and disabilities in particular. They see the blind man and ask Jesus, 'Rabbi, who sinned, this man or his parents, that he was born blind?' (9:2).

Ah, there it is. Our mental 'factory setting.' Like us, these disciples believed that things like disabilities had a fairly easy explanation – someone did something bad and got punished for it. This kind of thinking, ancient and modern, is a coping device. It helps us (we assume) make sense of why seemingly random suffering happens in a world overseen by a good God.

Their question reveals more than they intended. First, they have a wrong understanding of God and how He operates in this world. Now, as men raised in very religious Jewish culture, they should have known better. They knew the Old Testament well. They had read the book of Job, a central theme of which is an extended argument *against* this kind of thinking. They should have therefore known that this is not how God deals with us.

Their main assumption was that a disability like blindness was punishment for sin. They are thinking more like the Hindu worldview we covered in chapter 1 than men who were raised on the Old Testament Scriptures and what they say about God. They were recasting the God of the Bible into the human-sized god of karma.

In their minds – and ours, so often – the equation was straightforward. It was a simple deduction from mistaken and unbiblical premises – either this man sinned or his parents did. Therefore, God punished him. Karma wins. Simple.

Next, this understanding of God and how He works results in a mistaken view of themselves. Here's their reasoning: 'I'm probably not as bad as the blind man because, well, I'm not blind.' Karma wins. Again.

Notice how much we have in common with them. We want things kept simple. We don't want a God who is sovereign, even over disabilities. That kind of God would be unmanageable. Instead, we want a God who works the way we think He should.

Jesus' answer to His disciples should shock us. If you've been dozing off reading this chapter, His response should make you sit up. He replies, 'It was not that this man sinned, or his parents, but that the works of God might be displayed in him.' (9:3) No one expected this answer.

He goes on to explain what He means, but we can set that aside for the moment. We need to focus on this simple reply. It has two parts.

First, He draws His disciples back to this man's story. Jesus re-humanizes him to the disciples. Sin did not cause the blindness, either his or his parents'. In other words, get rid of your assumptions about God and yourselves. God does not punish people for their sins by giving them disabilities. Jesus is subtly telling them that they should know afflictions like blindness were the result of Adam's fall, not God's punishment.

Second, Jesus opens a door for us to understand God's ways. He says that this man was born blind so that the works of God might be displayed in him. In other words, God can use even something as difficult as a disability to show His power. 'Question your assumptions about God and yourselves,' is the basic message from Jesus in this episode.

GOD AND DISABILITIES

This snippet from John's Gospel can raise a lot of objections in our minds. Let's take a moment to work through what are likely the most urgent questions.

To my mind, the main question is, 'Why would God let this man be born blind?' The text gives us the answer – to display God's power. But that reply raises another, and maybe more difficult, question. 'What kind of a God would let this man suffer for so long just as an object lesson to the disciples?' Isn't there a better way to show His power?

As with some of the objections we considered above, this one assumes that God is arbitrary in the ways He governs our lives. But why believe that? Remember the Bible tells us we don't have the whole picture of our lives or world history. God does. And the Bible assures us that everything God does, He does for a reason.

In fact, God created reason and controls it, so the very fact that we even raise objections (based on *reasoning*) proves what we're trying to dismiss; namely the existence of a powerful and wise God. Put in a different way, our faculty of reasoning makes no sense on any other worldview except the one we find in the Bible.

For example, if we opt for a worldview which teaches that all is one, it follows that distinctions are illusions, as we saw in chapter 1. Yet, to reiterate what we argued there, for us to think about anything at all (including whether or not a worldview where all is one is true), we must draw distinctions. On this view of things, you use reason in order to deny reason. If you do some digging, I think you'll find the same thing for every other worldview apart from the one laid out in the Bible.

So our use of reason shows us that God exists. But that still doesn't answer the charge raised above; namely that God seems arbitrary in this passage. Why was this man born blind and not another?

If we understand that God's existence is necessary for us to reason at all, then it's fair to conclude that the God who gave us reason works in our lives in a *reasonable* way. That is to say, He is not arbitrary. Again, He had His reasons for allowing this man to be born blind, one of which was to show His glory. There were many other reasons which God did not tell us. The takeaway is that we can trust this reasonable God since the only alternative would be to deny reason altogether.

Finally, let's return to the question we asked above, 'Surely God could have shown His glory or done His work in some other way than this man being blind?' In other words, this question assumes that God would be unloving to show His power through suffering if He could have done it another way that didn't involve afflicting a person with blindness. How can God be good if blinding someone is how He chooses to show His power?

This objection wants to argue God is not good, maybe even immoral. The goodness or badness of actions, whether God's or ours, are inescapably moral questions. And all of us operate from some view of morals and what is right and wrong.

But we need to ask the same question of morality we just asked of reason. 'Which worldview can make sense of morality?'

The Bible assures us God is good and that His existence is the foundation of all human morality. There simply is no other worldview that can give us an ultimate standard by which to judge actions either good or evil. As with our faculty of reason, so with our moral convictions: even to argue against God's goodness requires the existence of the good God described in the Bible.

Applying this argument to the question before us, we can think this way. We may not be satisfied that God has good reasons for allowing this man to be born blind. But our dissatisfaction is not proof that God doesn't have good reasons; it just means we're dissatisfied! The real question is *why* are we dissatisfied? Dissatisfaction implies that something is not right, which, again, is a *moral* judgment. So even our dissatisfaction can be a kind of proof that God exists.

Here's a biblical example of what we're trying to understand. I mentioned the book of Job earlier. If you read that book, it opens with the 'backstory' – Satan comes to God and asks God's permission to afflict Job. We, the readers, have access to that backstory. Neither Job nor his friends did. So, they argue, back and forth, without having the full story. This is why the book ends with God asking Job a series of questions, all in service of showing him that questioning God's ways is unhelpful because Job didn't have all the facts.

Going back to the account in John 9, Jesus goes on to heal the man and this causes no small amount of controversy. The main takeaway is this. As with illnesses, God can heal disabilities, like He did for this man. But there is no guarantee that He will. So we must trust Him with our illnesses, our disabilities, and ultimately, in our death.

CONCLUSION

As we wrap up this chapter, I think the story of Joni Erickson Tada will provide a real-world example of someone who has suffered for a long time and still believes in Jesus. Not only does she believe in Him, but she also loves Him and serves many people in His name.

Her story is heartbreaking. When she was a teenager, she was paralyzed in a diving accident. From that time forward, she has been confined to a wheelchair. She cried out to God for healing and He did not answer in the way she asked. Most of us would be bitter against God in such circumstances.

But she wasn't and she isn't. Instead, she started a charity called Joni and Friends, which has done so much good around the world for people with disabilities. She explains,

> It's been costly and difficult to sit in this wheelchair for fifty-six years, but it's also been a blessing ... for me and for others. God took something that harmed my body (namely, my accident) and used it to not only give me Christ-centered hope and a future in eternity with Jesus – He also used it to give birth to Joni and Friends! And if sitting in this wheelchair all this time gives God more glory – if it advances the Gospel more quickly – then I am all for it![5]

I admit, I have a hard time imagining that I could have this kind of faith if my life were like hers. But her response inspires me. Instead of resentment towards God, she is full of hope and love. She understands deeply what Jesus

---

5. Joni Erickson Tada, 'God's Glorious Plan for My Life,' https://joniandfriends.org/posts-by-joni/gods-glorious-plan-for-my-life/, accessed April 1, 2024.

told His disciples in John's Gospel. She understands that God can use even a life-changing disability to bring glory to Himself. The question is, 'How?'

The answer we have studied in this chapter is that He can be trusted even in our most difficult afflictions. This is what Joni Erickson Tada learned. If we are willing to lay aside our assumptions about God and take Jesus at His word, like she did, we can have the hope and joy she has. Only the gospel can enable us to live like this.

5

What Does the Bible Say About Poverty and Abuse?

Greg LeMond is still the greatest American cyclist of all time. His win in the 1989 Tour de France by eight seconds is still the closest victory in the history of the world's premier bicycle race. My brothers and I love bike racing and my oldest brother was on the Champs Élysées that July day when LeMond triumphed over French cycling legend Laurent Fignon in the final time trial. 'Just amazing to be there and witness history being made,' he recalled.

LeMond would go on to win the 1990 Tour de France as well. From there, he launched a successful bike company and other business ventures. Buried under this flourishing career was a terrible secret that LeMond carried for years. He had been sexually abused when he was a child.

In the documentary about his life, *The Last Rider*, LeMond spoke about what this abuse did to him.

'Somehow you think you're responsible for it, or somehow you willingly participated in this thing, so that's part of the shame ... one day down the road, no matter where you are, it comes back to hit you.'[1] Of course, as LeMond goes on to explain, no abuse victim is responsible for it or willingly participated in it. But the shame that results from childhood sexual abuse is devastating and long-lasting – LeMond was in his sixties when he gave the interview I mentioned. The pain was still evident.

Abuse of any kind is evil. Whether emotional, sexual, physical, or otherwise, abuse leaves soul scars that may never heal. That's not to say that being emotionally abused is the same thing as being abused sexually. But it's also not to minimize any abuse you may have endured. The effects of abuse change us in ways we may not understand for years, but we feel their effects every day.

Poverty is another form of suffering that can have long-term effects. A few years ago, I was at supper with some friends, all of whom had done very well for themselves. When the server handed each of us the bill, everyone pulled out their wallets. One of the men in the group left a very, very large tip for this hard-working

---

1. *The Last Rider*, 20:59-22:15. Directed by Alex Holmes, performance by Perico Delgado, Laurent Fignon, Cyrille Guimard, Greg LeMond, and Kathy LeMond. Lions Gate Entertainment Corporation, 2022.

server. 'Why are you always outdoing us?' one of the others asked with a chuckle. My friend smiled in return and simply said, 'Because none of y'all have ever been poor. I have.'

Suffering either abuse or poverty or both will not leave us static. They will either drive us to God or farther away from Him.

In this chapter, we will study what the Bible says about these twin evils. As with the other topics we have surveyed, we'll see that the Bible is not silent on these issues. What it teaches us can benefit us enormously as we wrestle with these realities.

ABUSE

In general terms, the Bible makes it clear God hates it when those in power prey upon the weak and vulnerable. This is exactly what happens in any kind of abuse. In the Old Testament, the most common term to describe people in this condition is 'oppressed.' In the original Hebrew text, this word appears dozens of times and can mean affliction, defrauding, or doing violence against someone. (See, for example, passages like Lev.19:13; Deut. 24:14; Ps. 103:6.)

The most common categories for those who are weak and vulnerable are widows and orphans. Why these two? Because in a male-led, agrarian society, if a woman's husband or a child's father died, there were no government safety nets or social programs to help them. They were quite literally on their own. This is why the Old Testament has copious laws for the people of Israel to protect and care for the widows and orphans among them.

The same principle holds true in the New Testament. Jesus' half-brother, James, summarizes the Bible's teaching on how we are to help the weak and vulnerable: 'Religion that is pure and undefiled before God the Father is this: to visit orphans and widows in their affliction' (James 1:27).

Therefore, even though the Bible does not have any direct statements like, 'Thou shalt not abuse,' the terms and categories we just outlined make it clear that God hates any kind of abuse. He commands His people to care for the abused.

Moreover, the Bible warns us, in the strongest possible terms, of impending doom for those who abuse others. Representative of this awful threat are words from the prophet Malachi. 'I will draw near to you for judgment. I will be a swift witness against … those who oppress the hired worker in his wages, the widow and the fatherless, against those who thrust aside the sojourner, and do not fear me, says the LORD of hosts' (Mal. 3:5).

Thankfully, in the past few years, we have seen increased awareness about the pervasiveness of abuse. It is not a small problem. It is rampant. It needs to be exposed and prosecuted to the fullest possible extent of the law, where applicable.

Even with increased exposure and convictions of abusers, the emotional scar tissue does not heal easily, if ever. When we try to exercise the muscle of faith, that scar tissue inflames and causes our belief in God to atrophy. What can we do?

Once again, let's consider some of the main objections to God's goodness and justice when we encounter abuse of any kind. One argument I hear frequently is, 'There is no way a good God would allow child abuse if He could do something to stop it.' We saw a variation of this argument from Thomas Jay Oord in chapter 2.

It's a fair and difficult question. How can God be good if He could prevent the abuse of children and others but doesn't? This question hit me with force a few years ago. A woman who was not a member of the church I served came to see me and reported the details of horrible physical abuse at the hands of her husband. She contacted law enforcement as soon as the incident took place. But then the charges were dropped on a technicality. Panicked that her ex-husband was back on the streets, she pleaded, 'What can I do, when not even the police will protect me?' She felt hopeless and wondered if God really cared about her.

We can sympathize with her, can't we? If Christians proclaim that God is sovereign and good (as I have in this book), then why wouldn't a sovereign, all-powerful, all-loving God stop this man from abusing his wife?

An answer, as we said earlier, comes from two different perspectives. From the perspective of the here and now, I have no hesitation in saying, 'I don't know.' Let me immediately qualify that confession – I don't know *exhaustively* why God would not prevent child abuse. I add that qualifier because, as we'll see in a moment, I think we can know some reasons why. But, from the perspective of the here and now, I have to rest in the biblical truth that God's ways are not our ways (cf. Isaiah 55:8-9).

Now, at this level, this first perspective, we should also note that the alternative explanations aren't much help either. In other words, it's not just Christians who say, 'I don't know.' Atheism, other world religions, and just about every worldview will have to admit its limitations when it comes to this question.

So, there is an inescapable element of painful mystery to this question in particular and suffering in general. But not all mystery is created equal. Just because every worldview must admit its limitations does not mean we can't find a good answer to this question.

Viewed from a biblical perspective, we don't have to wring our hands and remain agnostic. We don't have to rest uncomfortably with 'I don't know.' We can say several things with certainty.

First, the Bible teaches that God's justice will ultimately prevail. This should comfort us enormously. Even if an abuser gets away with it in this life, the Bible teaches that this individual must still face God's judgment.

We might ask, 'Why does God take so long to accomplish justice?' The apostle Peter, one of Jesus' closest friends during His earthly ministry, gives us a ready answer.

> But do not overlook this one fact, beloved, that with the Lord one day is as a thousand years, and a thousand years as one day. The Lord is not slow to fulfill his promise as some count slowness, but is patient toward you, not wishing that any should perish, but that all should reach repentance. But the day of the Lord will come like a thief, and then the heavens will pass away with a roar, and the heavenly bodies will be burned up and dissolved, and the earth and the works that are done on it will be exposed. (2 Pet. 3:8-10)

This is a good summary of the Bible's teaching about God's timing and His justice. As I mentioned above, the Bible tells us that God's ways and timing are not the same as ours (cf. Isaiah 55:8-9). Peter also gives us the reason why God does not judge the earth swiftly. He is patient with us! His love is so vast that He wants to give us every chance possible to repent so that we will not face His terrifying wrath.

Someone might object, 'Do you mean to say that God wants child abusers to repent?' Yes, that is exactly what the text means. God wants *all* people to repent because if we don't, the Bible warns us about everlasting punishment.[2] Given that awful reality and given the fact that God detests the sin of abuse, it is amazing how patient God is with our sinfulness. If the abuser does not repent, then no earthly sentence will compare to the punishment He will endure – justly – at the hands of God.

This raises another question. 'Can we really still believe in something like a final judgment? With all that science has taught us, fire and brimstone and coming judgment sounds cartoonish.' To repurpose a line of reasoning from the previous chapter, if there is no ultimate justice from God, then how does the concept of justice in this life have any meaning? Think about it. If, as the scientific consensus teaches us, the universe will eventually dissolve into oblivion, which means there is no *ultimate* meaning to our lives, then there is no meaning to *anything* in the present.

---

2. For an excellent treatment of the difficult question of God's wrath and punishment, see the book in this series, Benjamin Skaug, *How Could a Loving God Send Anyone to Hell?* (Christian Focus, 2020).

This is true especially if one holds to the evolutionary worldview. We can easily spot some dire consequences with this way of thinking, if it is carried to its logical conclusion. I seriously doubt most evolutionists would make this case, but if natural selection is true, then someone could argue that abuse might be a helpful action in service of natural selection. For, if the strong abuse the weak, with the result that the weaker members of the human 'herd' are culled out, then maybe abuse is a good thing for survival. As I said, this is perverse reasoning. But it would be consistent, given evolutionary presuppositions.

This isn't a theoretical example. In 2001, the prestigious Massachusetts Institute of Technology Press published a scholarly book by two scientists entitled *A Natural History of Rape*.[3] I think all readers would agree rape is a form of abuse and is always wrong. These authors also agree and their argument is pretty straightforward. They assure readers that rape is a criminal act and therefore wrong. But they also point out that rape (which is almost always perpetrated by males) stems from the evolutionary sex drive. So, they recommend certain ways

---

3. Randy Thornhill and Craig T. Palmer, *A Natural History of Rape: Biological Bases of Sexual Coercion* (Boston: MIT Press, 2001). Consult chapters 1, 3, and 11 for their argument summarized above.

145

to curb this instinct in males. To repeat, they believe rape is wrong. But they also believe that rape is *natural*, given evolutionary views on human sexuality.

Do you see the problem? The authors want to make a moral claim (rape is wrong), while being compelled by their evolutionary presuppositions to admit that nature is amoral. But if all that happens in nature, including rape, happens because of evolutionary impulses, which are amoral, then how can we make any moral judgments about anything, including rape?

I am grateful that these authors did not conclude that rape was a helpful evolutionary mechanism. But I struggle to see how they could prevent someone from drawing that conclusion if that person believes in the evolutionary paradigm. If nature is all there is, then there is no transcendent basis for morality. And if there is no transcendent basis for morality, then whatever happens just happens. We can't say it's right or wrong.

All that to say, if we accept any kind of evolutionary worldview, then there are only a couple of options in front of us when it comes to making sense of the lack of justice in this life. On the evolutionary view, we can't even speak meaningfully of justice, since there is nothing and no one outside of nature to provide a sufficient grounding of moral judgments like justice. So this answer cannot make sense of the lack of justice.

On the other hand, the Bible teaches that there *is* final justice because there is a Judge, the triune God. Because this is true, we can not only make sense of the lack of justice we receive in this life, we can also know for certain that all injustice will be put right in the end.

Knowing this is true helps us in the case of someone like Greg LeMond. He suffered years of abuse and the person that committed these crimes died without receiving any punishment. This is a massive injustice. But, on the Christian worldview, we can know that, even if someone like LeMond's abuser escaped justice in this life, he will still have to face the Judge of everyone, God Himself.

What about God's goodness? How can God be good if He has the power to prevent abuse but doesn't? This question takes us back to what we saw in chapter 2, namely that God must have a morally sufficient reason for the evil we experience, even if we cannot discern that reason. As we saw, this answer helps us make sense of the *logical* problem of personal evil and suffering. But what about the *personal* problem of suffering and evil, especially when it comes to something as awful as abuse?

In reality, we must have this logical answer straight in our minds before we can experience personal healing from evils like abuse. In other words, the logical answer and our personal experience are intertwined. How? Well, if we know that God has a morally sufficient reason for our suffering, we can begin to trust Him. We can know our suffering is not arbitrary. We can know that He is not the author of our suffering. In short, we can know that He is still good despite our experience.

We also need to be clear that the Bible does not teach that abuse victims should stay with those who abuse them. This point mainly applies to domestic abuse. Too many of us are aware of the sad reality that many women who are abused by men feel trapped in these kinds of relationships. Some have even been taught that the Bible commands women to stay with their husbands, no matter what. This is not true.

Space forbids a lengthy treatment of why this is the case, so I'll have to refer you to other sources for a fuller discussion.[4] The basic answer is that the Bible tells us that marriage is a covenant between a man and a woman (Gen. 2:21-25; Eph. 5:25ff). Abuse is a violation of that covenant, which renders it null and void. Therefore, when abuse occurs in a marriage or a home, God commands us to seek whatever legal or immediate protection we need

---

4. The denomination in which I serve, the Presbyterian Church in America, recently empaneled a group of experts, from both inside and outside the church, to study this issue. Their extensive report offers invaluable insights, not only on the causes of abuse, but how to prevent it and how to care for those who have been abused. You can access it at https://pcaga.org/aic-report-abuse/

to ensure that it stops. Moreover, He does not require us to stay in an abusive relationship.

To sum up, the Bible teaches us that abuse is always wrong. It teaches us that God will punish abusers, unless they repent of this sin. It calls upon us to seek out help from law enforcement, pastors, or counselors when we have been abused. And it assures us that God can bring good even out of the evil of abuse.

Poverty

Like every other topic in this book, poverty has been a problem since humans began recording history. And like abuse, if we experience poverty it will make us question God's justice and goodness. So how, then, does the Bible teach us to think about poverty? Let's begin looking at this issue in general terms.

A distinguished economist did a presentation at our church a few months ago. She was helping us consider ways we could best help the poor. During her slide show, she displayed a graph that I think most people found surprising. It showed the massive, historic decline of worldwide poverty over the past 100 years. That's good news! Nations are getting wealthier and the standard of living is increasing across the board.[5]

---

5. A representative article which documents this trend is François Bourguignon and Christian Morrisson, 'Inequality among

Still, as I write this, inflation is at an all-time high. Lots of people I know are living paycheck to paycheck. Roughly thirty-seven million people in the US live below the poverty line.[6] Despite all the progress we see around the world, poverty is still a significant problem.

Jesus says something very interesting about the issue of poverty. 'The poor you [will] always have with you' (John 12:8). Jesus did not say this callously; you'll search in vain through the annals of history to find someone who cared more about the poor than Jesus. No, He is not callous; since He is God in the flesh, He is echoing what the Lord said to His people in the Old Testament about the nature of poverty and their duty to care for the poor. 'For there will never cease to be poor in the land. Therefore I command you, "You shall open wide your hand to your brother, to the needy and to the poor, in your land"' (Deut. 15:11).

Verses like these are representative of the Bible's vast teaching on poverty. It teaches us that poverty will always be a problem because people are sinners. But God cares

---

World Citizens 1820–1992,' *American Economic Review* 92, no.4 (2002): pp. 727-44. My thanks to Dr. Claudia Williamson Kramer for drawing my attention to this source.

6. Emily A. Shrider and John Creamer, 'Poverty in the United States: 2022,' https://www.census.gov/library/publications/2023/demo/p60-280.html#:~:text=Highlights-,Official%20Poverty%20Measure,and%20Table%20A%2D1), accessed March 15, 2024.

for the poor, as He tells us countless times in the Bible. Additionally, He expects His people to care for the poor.

The truth is that Christians have done a lot for the poor in obedience to Jesus' command to care for those in need. In fact, it was Christianity that made helping the poor a standard maxim in Western culture. No other worldview provides the necessary underpinnings that have resulted in the prosperity Western culture has enjoyed for centuries. That prosperity, in turn, led to a higher standard of living across the board for all people in Western societies, including the poor.[7]

With this background, let's dive into some of the questions that arise, whether we experience poverty ourselves or wrestle with how much of it still remains in the world. I imagine all of us have seen the images of people around the world starving to death. Who can see such pictures and remain uncaring? Circumstances like these force us to ask, 'Why does God allow so much poverty to continue in the world?'

We can say a few things in response. First, much of the global poverty we see is a result of rampant corruption in so many of these countries that desperately

---

7. For an in-depth exploration of these facts from a non-Christian scholar, see Rodney Stark, *The Victory of Reason: How Christianity Led to Freedom, Capitalism, and Western Success* (New York: Random House, 2006).

need material aid. Why would God allow that to be the case? As we have seen, He has given us the freedom to choose according to our desires. Unfortunately, a lot of people desire money above all else. They are greedy, simply put. If we scale greed to national levels, we have major problems on our hands. In biblical language, much of the worldwide poverty we witness is a result of human sinfulness.

Second, sometimes God permits poverty in order to give people with resources an opportunity to help those in need. He is committed to making sure His people do not trust money instead of Him. So He commands them to be generous with their material wealth. 'As for the rich in this present age, charge them not to be haughty, nor to set their hopes on the uncertainty of riches, but on God, who richly provides us with everything to enjoy' (1 Tim. 6:17).

As you can see, God expects churches and individuals to be committed to helping the poor. The verse above makes it clear that wealth is not evil; only the love of wealth is evil (1 Tim. 6:10). And one of the main reasons God gives wealth to people is for them to give it to those who do not have it. They are to do this willingly, because their hope is in God, not in money.

So far we have been discussing poverty in general terms. Maybe a more painful question for you is, 'Why doesn't God remove poverty in my life? If He cares for me and has promised to provide for me, why don't I see that happening?' These are gut-wrenching questions, but the Bible does provide us good answers.

First, we need to be honest with ourselves. Sometimes our poverty is a result of our choices. Think about how easy it is to find ourselves with crushing debt, which robs us from growing our wealth or getting out of poverty. Everything around us is calculated to make us covetous of things we don't have. For example, the bulk of the advertising industry, which exercises so much influence in our lives, was created to make us desire things we don't yet possess.

Therefore, we spend and spend to get things and find ourselves swimming in debt. We make choices to spend the way we do based on our desires. So we need to do the hard work of looking at how we use our money and, more importantly, *why* we spend our money the way we do. Our desires can land us in poverty. The solution here is to repent of these desires and commit our lives to Jesus and following Him. He will change our desires so that we can put our material resources to use in ways that will not only help us out of poverty but, most importantly, honor God.

There is a larger problem at this point, though. Millions of people are *born* into poverty. That is, they experience poverty because of *other* peoples' sinful choices and not their own. This seems so unfair. But notice that choice works in both directions. That is, even if poverty is not a result of our choices, we can still make decisions that will lead us out of poverty. Let me illustrate.

One of my colleagues at the church I currently serve grew up extremely poor in an inner city of New Jersey. He wrote a book about his experience, which I think anyone concerned with questions we have raised in this chapter should read.

He became a Christian as a teenager and was eventually called to the ministry. From there, he started a church in Chattanooga in the early 1970s dedicated to preaching the gospel and helping the poor. The church grew and continues its mission today. It has quite literally changed our city. In addition to this one church, my colleague also started a worldwide network of churches with the same mission (which is just the mission of Jesus!) and they are a multi-continental vibrant force for preaching the gospel and helping people suffering with poverty.[8]

In his book, he tells the story of how he got out of generational poverty. The biggest change in his life was a change of worldview, as we have discussed throughout

---

8. I am referring to the New City Network. You can learn more about this important ministry at their website: https://thenewcitynetwork.org

this book. He came to believe the Bible's teaching on God, sin, forgiveness, and redemption – the gospel. He embraced Jesus as his Savior and the biblical worldview that Jesus teaches us.

Importantly, my friend also talks about how it wasn't just good theology (though that is indispensable!) that lifted him out of poverty. It was good theology *lived out* by a mentor in his life, a pastor.[9] In our lives, it might be a pastor, a coach, a teacher, or a mentor who shows us a way out of generational poverty.

No matter who the person is, we still must know the causes and cures of poverty. As my friend argues in his book, only the Bible can help us here. Since it gives us the true story of reality, any solutions for poverty not based on the Bible will fail us.

These observations lead us to a final question on this subject. Why, if I work hard and do not spend beyond my means, do I still experience poverty, if God cares for me? I'll let my colleague give a better answer than I could.

> Behind all our circumstances is His unseen hand at work to bring about His will. This idea can create resentment toward God and the teachings of the

---

9. My colleague is Rev. Randy Nabors. See his book *Merciful: The Opportunity and Challenge of Discipling the Poor Out of Poverty* (North Charleston, SC: CreateSpace Independent Publishing, 2015), pp. 24-25. He spends a large portion of this work detailing proven solutions from the Bible that help people out of poverty.

Bible. In my case, however, it gave a sense of relief. In other words, this truth told me my family's poverty had a purpose, and for me it provided a great comfort. So you might understand clearly, I am saying God sovereignly planned for my family to be poor – and in retrospect I am thankful for it ... whether one agrees or not with the theology or philosophy of this idea (destiny, predestination, etc.) it will not change the reality as to whether God is behind things or not.[10]

Those are some strong words! But they make sense don't they? As he points out, whether we believe or disbelieve in the sovereignty of God does not change the reality of this truth. We can either let God's sovereignty comfort us or drive us away from Him. And, as my friend's experience shows, if we choose to follow Jesus and obey His commands to help the poor, He can take our suffering and use it for good in ways we could never imagine.

CONCLUSION

The subjects we have discussed in this chapter are difficult indeed. But I hope that the Bible's answers will bring you some comfort if you are experiencing them. As with the other topics in this book, we may not have all the answers

---

10. Nabors, *Merciful,* p. 50.

to abuse or poverty, but we do have God's promise to be with us as we suffer. Likewise, we have people like my friend who provide us real-world examples who demonstrate that the theological and logical answers we have discussed really do help us in our daily lives. As a result, we can trust God, even if we have suffered things like abuse and poverty. That's really good news.

6

But What About … ?

Up to this point, we have worked through some specific instances of personal suffering and evil. I have tried to answer objections to Christianity that arise when we undergo these trials. In this chapter, I want to summarize these objections more broadly. We'll look at six questions that cover the principal difficulties we have discussed.[1]

Question 1

DOESN'T MY SUFFERING MEAN THAT GOD ISN'T IN CONTROL?

Throughout this book, we have returned to the bedrock truth of God's sovereign control over our suffering and evil. Even so, we still wonder, 'How can we *know* God is sovereign?' After all, we can't test the doctrine of

---

1. I am grateful to Greg Welty for suggesting these questions.

God's sovereignty in a laboratory. We can't confirm it through a series of empirical procedures. This question, therefore, highlights the truth that our worldview matters. In other words, as C. S. Lewis reminded us in chapter 4, the *philosophical assumptions* we bring to our experience will determine whether or not we will believe God.

So how can we know God is sovereign? As I have tried to point out along the way, we must embrace the biblical worldview. At the core of this worldview is the teaching that God is both sovereign *and* good. Given these twin realities, we would *expect* this sovereign, good God to work through our suffering. In other words, if the Bible teaches us to expect God to work through our suffering (consider the biblical examples we have offered throughout this book), then our suffering can't be evidence God is not in control.

Of course, many people believe that the biblical worldview is too irrational to be taken seriously. To be blunt, this kind of thinking really is blind faith, for it rules out the Bible's teaching before even taking the time to investigate it. But is that a reasonable way to go through life, especially when we are considering something as painful as suffering and evil in our experience? I don't think so. Moreover, as we have seen, embracing the biblical worldview does not mean that we must choose between reason or faith. There are good reasons to believe that the Bible is true. The kind of faith the Bible invites us to exercise is not a blind leap in the dark. It is the most rational choice we could make.

To see why this is the case, let's return to another point we made in chapter 4. Even to make use of reason presupposes that the biblical worldview is true. As we saw there, God discloses Himself as the creator, redeemer, and sustainer of everything in the universe. He created order and regularity in this world, the necessary preconditions for reason. When we dig into other worldviews, religions, and philosophies, we find that they cannot offer a rational explanation for our daily experience, let alone our suffering and evil.

Someone might object, 'Yes, but you can't possibly investigate every religion or philosophy. So maybe there's a better explanation than the Christian worldview. We just haven't discovered it yet.'

I agree in one sense – there is no way finite humans can ever know every possible philosophy or religion that may arise. But notice *this objection is simply another kind of faith*. It prefers to withhold belief in the Christian worldview in favor of a truly blind leap of faith; namely, 'Maybe something better than the biblical worldview will come along in the future.'

Think about it – there is no *evidence* for this alternative worldview that will supposedly offer a better explanation. It is purely theoretical, a kind of desperate escape hatch. By contrast, we have all kinds of evidence for the truthfulness of Christianity, not the least of which is that the worldview offered by the Bible can make sense not only of our suffering, but also of everything else.

If the Christian worldview offers us not only intellectually satisfying answers, but also a loving Savior, what sense does it make to reject this worldview and wait for something supposedly better? At some point, we're going to have to admit that there really are no good reasons to doubt the Bible's teachings if those doubts have been addressed. Sure, we can keep inventing theoretical objections, but we still have to live our daily lives which, as we said at the outset of this study, will always involve suffering.

Also, don't overlook the fact that all of us are living out a worldview *right now*. We may claim to be waiting for something better than the biblical worldview, but none of us can suspend our beliefs completely; we all consider some things incontestable and certain. The question again is, 'Why trust those beliefs if they can be shown to be rationally deficient?' Put more simply, as I heard one minister say, 'Doubt your doubts about Christianity.'

Question 2

*DOESN'T MY SUFFERING TEACH ME THAT
THERE IS NO POINT TO HISTORY?*

If suffering and evil make our lives feel senseless and hopeless, they also seem to make history pointless. If we adopt this view, then history is just a random mixture of good and evil. But it's worse than that – history seems to demonstrate the veracity of nineteenth-century poet Alfred, Lord Tennyson's observation that 'nature is red in tooth and claw.'[2] In other words, evil and suffering seem to far outweigh good in human experience, which can lead us to conclude that history is pointless.

But, as we've seen, no one can live out this belief consistently. Well, that's not quite right – the only way to live this kind of philosophy consistently is to take one's own life. That may sound outrageously harsh and offensive, but let me explain.

Suicide is the natural result of this line of thinking. If history is pointless and life is meaningless, then why go on? To be clear, most people are not consistent with their most basic presuppositions. Particularly in this instance, we can be very grateful for such inconsistency.

---

2. Alfred, Lord Tennyson, 'In Memoriam A.H.H.,' https://www.online-literature.com/tennyson/718/, Canto 56, accessed August 1, 2024.

This is not just my opinion. People like Raïssa Maritain, the celebrated poet and wife of the philosopher Jacques Maritain, have understood that suicide is the only way to be consistent with the assumption that history is pointless. She details a pact she and Professor Maritain made when they came to believe life and history were pointless.

> Thus we decided for some time longer to have confidence in the unknown; we would extend credit to existence, look upon it as an experiment to be made, in the hope that to our ardent pleas, the meaning of life would reveal itself, that new values would stand forth so clearly that they would enlist our total allegiance, and deliver us from the nightmare of a sinister and useless world. But if the experiment should not be successful, the solution would be suicide; suicide before the years had accumulated their dust, before our youthful strength was spent.[3]

We can admire the Maritains' philosophical consistency, even as we recoil at the logic that forced them to arrive at such a horrific conclusion. Mercifully, neither followed through with their plans. In fact, both became Christians.

So, what we believe about the meaning (or lack thereof) of history and, specifically, the evil and suffering

---

3. Raïssa Maritain, *The Memoirs of Raïssa Maritain* (Image Books 1961), pp. 65-68; cited in Steve Hays, *This Joyful Eastertide: A Critical Review of the Empty Tomb* (e-book, 2006), p. 21.

the human race experiences in history, will have far-reaching consequences for our lives. What I have tried to show is that the Christian worldview offers us a true story that provides meaning for our suffering. It teaches us that God made all things good, that man sinned against God, which brought about all the suffering and evil in our lives and in world history, and that God has acted to redeem His creation and put an end to everything that is opposed to Him, including suffering and evil.

Once we embrace this story and make it our own, we can begin to experience the reality of God's love, even in our trials – maybe *especially* then. Why? Because at the heart of the biblical story of God's love is an instrument of suffering, the cross.

This, then, is the life pattern of the Christian, given to us by Jesus Himself. Suffering, then glory. The cross, then the crown. This order is irreversible. Understood in this light, the suffering and evil we experience are not meaningless; they have a grand purpose in a grand story, at the heart of which is God Himself taking on human nature, so that He could suffer *for* us and suffer *with* us.

The apostle Paul knew this to be the case. He suffered tremendously during his life (see 2 Corinthians 11:23-29 for a partial list of some of the calamities that befell him). Yet, because he knew his suffering was sent to him by the sovereign, sympathetic Savior, he could write triumphantly, 'This light momentary affliction is preparing for us an eternal weight of glory beyond all comparison' (2 Cor 4:17).

According to the apostle here, we can move from a place in our lives where personal suffering and evil undo us to a place where we can say that whatever comes to us is 'light' and 'momentary' because all of it is preparation for coming glory. The gospel alone provides us the resilience we need to endure the hardships of life because it alone offers us a Savior who has experienced every difficulty we will ever face and triumphed over them all. When we suffer, we will find a sympathetic, understanding Savior who will never abandon us in our trials.

Question 3

*DOESN'T MY SUFFERING PROVE THAT GOD
IS UNINTERESTED IN MY WELFARE?*

The previous answer leads us to another objection. If God allows me to suffer so much, He must not be interested in my welfare. Is that true? Not at all. While we focused on the cross of Jesus above, the Bible teaches us that Jesus' cross is inseparable from His resurrection. God is so interested in our welfare and eternal salvation that He not only sent Jesus to die in our place, He also raised Him from the dead. Here is another biblical pattern which we will discover in our daily lives – death then resurrection.

Here's what I mean. Every suffering we undergo is a kind of 'mini-death.' It takes something from us, just like death will ultimately claim our lives. However, because of Jesus' resurrection, in the midst of a thousand mini-deaths we can experience just as many 'mini-resurrections.' In other words, the suffering and evil in our lives cause us to re-enact the gospel *daily*. One author describes this dynamic in simple terms. 'Jesus' death was once for all … mine was ongoing.'[4] He concludes, 'We experience [Jesus'] resurrection now as His Spirit inhabits our *spirits*, helping us to see all of life through a resurrection lens. Because it's His resurrection that we are participating in, we can enjoy resurrection now as we wait for the final resurrection … resurrection is the final word.'[5]

Read that last line again: resurrection is the final word. Not death. Not suffering. Not evil. The Holy Spirit enables us to see resurrection in our lives, even as we experience mini-deaths. In sum, we can have resurrection life in the midst of our daily deaths.

This pattern reminds us of bedrock truth #5, the Spirit is strong. Since Jesus was raised from the dead

---

4. Paul E. Miller, *The J-Curve: Dying and Rising with Jesus in Everyday Life* (Wheaton, IL: Crossway, 2019), p. 30. I am also indebted to Miller's work for the language of mini-death and mini-resurrection.

5. Ibid., p. 212; emphasis original.

and ascended into heaven, now the Holy Spirit, the third person of the Trinity, who is also God, indwells us (John 16:7; Rom 8:9). The Holy Spirit enables us to press on in hope through our sufferings, as He empowers us to re-enact the gospel of dying and rising in our lives.

All of this teaches us how passionately God is interested in our welfare. The Father loves us so deeply that He sends His Son to live, die, and rise in our place. The Father and the Son send the Spirit to indwell us and make sure our sufferings do not wreck us. All three persons of the Trinity work for our welfare. Again, no other worldview offers such a believable, rational explanation not only for our suffering, but also of God's astounding love for us when we suffer. Why? Because, unlike the other gods, Jesus suffered when He walked this earth. No other worldview offers us a God who can sympathize with us in our trials.

Question 4

WON'T MY SUFFERING INEVITABLY MAKE ME WORSE AS A HUMAN BEING?

Over the course of our study, we have read about numerous people who suffered terribly and yet were drawn closer to God in their hardships. Remember Helen Roseveare or my colleague I mentioned in chapter 5. Stories like these could be multiplied many times over.

On the other hand, all of us know people who have become bitter and resigned because of their suffering. These two different outcomes remind us that we have a choice when we suffer. We can choose to believe what God tells us or we can choose to believe something else. I would submit to you that, considering all that we have learned, if you choose any other way but God's way, then suffering will make you cynical and depressed. It will, in fact, make you worse as a human being.

By contrast, the Bible teaches us that, if we believe in Jesus, the suffering and evil we experience have at least two outcomes in our lives, both of which will make us better people. First, these things humble us. Second, they sanctify us. Since that second term may be unfamiliar to you, let's look at these two in reverse order, beginning with the fact that suffering sanctifies us.

The word *sanctify* comes from a Latin word which means to 'set apart.' In the Bible, sanctification refers to the process whereby God sets us apart from a life of sin to make us more like Jesus. Paul's words to the Romans on this subject summarize the Bible's teaching in one verse. 'But now that you have been set free from sin and have become slaves of God, the fruit you get leads to sanctification and its end, eternal life' (Rom. 6:22). Being a 'slave to God' means being a follower of Jesus. When that happens, sanctification begins.

Following Jesus means we will suffer, as we saw above, but also that we will not suffer alone. This is why Paul could write, 'Now I rejoice in my sufferings for your sake, and in my flesh I am filling up what is lacking in Christ's afflictions' (Col. 1:24). Paul was not saying that Jesus' sufferings for us were not enough to atone for our sins. Far from it. No, he is telling us that we can come to a place of rejoicing in our sufferings precisely because we do not suffer alone. We suffer in union with Christ, and this is part of the sanctification process.

Of course, this does not mean we should go looking for suffering. God is not a masochist! Instead, we should receive whatever suffering comes our way knowing at least two things at once: 1) God loves me and has a plan for my life that includes suffering, and 2) God will use my suffering to sanctify me and my sanctification happens because I am united to Christ by faith.

The suffering and evil we experience also humble us. Few of us admit or even recognize how basic pride is to every aspect of our lives. For example, you may not walk around telling others how great you are (our typical image of a proud person), but we are still proud people. A simple illustration will demonstrate this uncomfortable truth.

Take stock of your thoughts when you must wait as you go about your day. It may be in traffic, in a line at the store, or even just for a web page to load on your phone. Watch how quickly you find yourself getting impatient. 'That's only natural,' you might say. That may be true, but that doesn't make impatience right. The real question is *why* do we get impatient so easily?

The Bible tells us that the simple answer to this question is *pride*. In our sinfulness, we want the world to run our way. We want our plans to come to pass. Something as trivial as waiting in line reveals our proud hearts when our pseudo-sovereign plans are frustrated. We want our lives to go our way, all the time. This is the height of pride.

Our suffering and the evil that befalls us are both constant reminders of some pride-destroying truths: We are not God. We are not sovereign. We do not understand all He is doing.

I realize that these statements may seem cruel, especially if you're undergoing a painful time in your life. But God wants to humble us for a very simple reason. It is only when we let go of our pretended claims to deity – the height of pride – that we will experience God's care for us in our suffering. Pride will keep us from God, and humility will always draw us closer to God.

So, returning to our original question, will suffering make me worse as a human being? Not if we humble ourselves and realize that God's process of sanctification will actually make us *fully* human. Why? Because our sufferings conform us to Christ, the paradigm of true humanity.

Question 5

IF THE CHRISTIAN LIFE INVOLVES SUFFERING, WHY SHOULD ANYONE CONTINUE IN IT?

I think this is one of the most important questions we will ever ask. Popular teaching from misguided Christians tells us that Jesus wants His followers to be healthy and wealthy. However, as we have seen, that's not what the New Testament teaches. Instead, it tells us that the Christian life is one of 'losses and crosses,' as some of the older Christian writings used to put it.

So why keep going? Because of what God has promised. He has told us that if we surrender our lives to Jesus, then we will have treasure in heaven (Matt. 19:21). He tells us that we have a magnificent inheritance – the new heavens and the new earth which Jesus will usher in at His return, a world free from pain and suffering, overflowing with goodness and joy. It will be a place that is restored both physically and spiritually. As a friend of mine likes to put it, heaven will not be a low-calorie affair!

Over and over, the Bible reminds us how fleeting this life is and how much we stand to lose if we reject God's gracious offer of salvation. It also reminds us how much we stand to gain if we follow Jesus, even if that means suffering and trials for His sake.

Consider the alternative. As I mentioned in chapter 5, the Bible does not take sin lightly. It teaches us, in no uncertain terms, that God's just judgment will fall on anyone who does not repent and believe in Jesus as their personal Lord and Savior. I don't write that with any kind of glee or triumph. Frankly, the reality of everlasting condemnation is something so sad, so terrible to contemplate, that I do not like thinking about it at all.

But the Bible forces us to grapple with this awful reality. If you're still skeptical about all of this, let me encourage you to read any one of the four Gospels. Notice how often Jesus spells out the dire consequences of rejecting Him. Was He doing this because He was an egomaniac? Hardly. He spoke of these things because He loves us and wants all of us to come to Him and avoid this tragic fate.

Back to our original question. Why keep going? In a word, because of all the good things God has promised us and because the alternative – everlasting condemnation – is too high a price to consider, let alone pay, just to avoid the suffering that is inherent in the Christian life.

Above all, we should not serve God simply for what we can get from Him. That would be using God. No one likes to feel used. Instead of using God in this way, the

Bible shows us that God is our highest good. In other words, He promises us joy and gladness and so many good things if we trust Jesus, but He Himself is the best gift of all. God Himself is our inheritance! Everything good that comes with that unimaginable inheritance is just the icing on the cake, so to speak.

Question 6

Isn't every Christian alone in his suffering?

Finally, let's consider a topic we haven't spent much time thinking about in this book: suffering in community. One of the most comforting provisions from God for me when I suffer is to know that I am not alone. I have my church family, and I have the church family of the past and present, through their writings, to help me when I want to give up.

We moderns do not suffer well. This is chiefly because we have alleviated so much of our suffering in so many areas – and this is a good thing, as we saw in chapter 3. So we are shocked by suffering when it comes into our lives. This being the case, we can learn much from those who have suffered well, both past and present.

When evil and suffering have come into my life, I have found great comfort in the writings of the Puritans of the sixteenth and seventeenth centuries. Who were the Puritans? They were a group of Christians who lived in this time who were committed to purity of worship, meaning that they did not agree with the state-enforced prescriptions for worship. In fact, the word 'Puritan' was originally coined as a term of derision by their opponents. Despite massive opposition, however, the Puritans were men, women, boys, and girls whose commitment to God would put most modern Christians to shame.

Now, if your mental picture of a Puritan is a joyless, hard taskmaster, clad in black and seeking out the next witch to burn, realize that this popular caricature is just that – a distorted fiction.[6] In reality, the Puritans were some of the most resilient, joyful people you will find in history. And they suffered greatly.

Therefore, we can learn much from them. Almost all of them buried multiple children and spouses, were persecuted and even killed for their faith, and lived their lives under constant threat of state-sanctioned penalties. Despite these adversities, they wrote lengthy treatises on the love of God and the joy of following Jesus. That is, their terrible suffering did not make them doubt the biblical truths we have discussed in this book.

---

6. Professor Leland Ryken's painstaking study of the Puritans demonstrates just how distorted are the scholarly and popular conceptions of Puritans. See Leland Ryken, *Worldly Saints: The Puritans as They Really Were* (Grand Rapids, MI: Zondervan, 1986).

To be sure, I'm not trying to paper over their glaring faults. Like all of us, the Puritans were sinners and even as they suffered well, they also failed miserably. Yet, when we look over the course of Christian history, we will be hard-pressed to find a group that can teach us more about suffering well.

One example will have to suffice. John Flavel (1628–91) was an English Puritan whose first wife died giving birth to their first child, who also died. He married again and his second wife also died. A devout minister, he was forced from his pulpit in 1662 because of the Act of Uniformity, which stipulated that all Protestants in England had to use the Book of Common Prayer in their worship. He refused and was forced to preach in secret meetings. In short, his life was full of suffering.

But it was not joyless. Why? Because he understood bedrock truth #1, God is sovereign. So convinced was he of this truth that he wrote a book about it, *The Mystery of Providence*. In that work, he describes how Christians will one day understand something of God's designs in our sufferings. 'All the dark, intricate, puzzling providences at which we were sometimes so offended, and sometimes amazed, which we could neither reconcile with the promise [of God] nor with each other, nay, which we so unjustly censured and bitterly bewailed, we shall then see to be to us, as the difficult passage through the wilderness was to Israel, "the right way to a city of habitation" (Ps. 107:7).'[7]

In simple terms, Flavel is telling us that one day we will understand something of God's purposes in our lives. He compares our lives to Israel in the wilderness on the way to the promised land. By doing this, he reminds us that in this wilderness life we will suffer and that we will never be alone when we do. For, just as God guided Israel safely through the wilderness, He will guide us safely through our own wildernesses. Flavel believed this knowledge should give us unshakable hope in God's goodness even when we are suffering.

I'll close with a much more recent example. Katherine Wolf and her husband were married in 2004 and moved to L.A. for him to begin law school. She was an aspiring model and actress with a promising career. They were living the dream of so many young married couples – happy, healthy, and enjoying life.

All that changed on April 21, 2008. Katherine's husband came home to find her face down on the floor. She had suffered an extremely rare stroke caused by a birth defect. Her life was changed forever.

The stroke was just the beginning of extreme physical suffering. Five years later, doctors removed a

---

7. John Flavel, *The Mystery of Providence*, (Carlisle, PA: The Banner of Truth Trust, 2009 [1678]), p. 22.

brain aneurysm. After that, she was diagnosed with a neurovascular disease. In short, Katherine Wolf's life is full of anguish she never anticipated.

But she has continued to trust Jesus throughout these trials. In her recent book, *Treasures in the Dark*, she reflects on her pain and offers the perspective we all need when life-altering circumstances strike us out of the blue.

> The darkest days of my suffering had taught me things that a pain-free life never could have. In the darkness, I experienced peace that transcended my circumstances. I rediscovered my worth apart from my ability. I gave up the illusion that I was in control of much of anything. None of that could have happened in a life lived exclusively in the light of favorable circumstances. When I redefined darkness as the place in which God's light can shine most brightly, I didn't have to be so afraid of suffering and sorrow anymore.[8]

Wolf goes on to explain that she still struggles in her faith, still has very dark days, and still questions God. But she keeps going, entrusting her suffering to Jesus even when she doesn't understand.

CONCLUSION

The kind of resilience exemplified by Flavel and Wolf can become our new normal when we suffer. Even when we

---

8. Katherine Wolf, *Treasures in the Dark: 90 Reflections on Finding Bright Hope Hidden in the Hurting* (Nashville, TN: W Publishing Group, an imprint of Thomas Nelson, 2024), xii.

don't understand why we are afflicted, we can continue to have hope. We can rise above our suffering and find light in the darkness. How? By following the same path these two Christians traveled and found hope – the difficult but not therefore joyless path of following Jesus. This is the only road that leads to resurrection, both the 'mini-resurrections' in our daily lives and the final glorious resurrection of the life to come.

7

Life in the Gap

The central claim of this book is that our most fundamental beliefs about reality – our worldview – will exercise a controlling influence over how we deal with personal suffering and evil. To that end, I have argued that the biblical worldview provides us not only an intellectually satisfying understanding of our difficulties, but also a way of thinking that can help us flourish when we face life's hardships. In other words, I have tried to show that theology is practical. True theology can help us when we suffer. False theology offers us no help at all.

A distinctive teaching of the Bible's theology is the tension between what God has promised and what we experience in the here and now. That is, the Bible records countless promises of how God will bless His people, save them, and care for them. It also tells us that there will be a gap between promise and fulfillment. All of us are living in that gap right now.

As we finish our study, I want to explore this gap a bit further. I believe the Bible's claims about life in this gap will provide enormous comfort to us when we suffer. If we understand that what God has promised and what we experience do not mean that God has failed us, we can move away from skepticism and cynicism and towards Him in faith.

THE PRINCIPAL BIBLICAL PATTERN: PROMISE AND FULFILLMENT

Let's begin by sketching the biblical *pattern* for understanding history. Since God created the world and humanity fell into sin, He has been making promises. The first comes in Genesis 3:15, right after the fall of Adam and Eve: 'I will put enmity between you and the woman, and between your offspring and her offspring; he shall bruise your head, and you shall bruise his heel.' God is speaking to Satan in this context, telling the devil that he will be defeated ultimately.

This might be the most important promise in all the Bible. As one of my pastors put it once, everything that follows in the Bible – everything in the remaining sixty-five books – is a footnote to this verse, since Genesis 3:15 gives us a summary of world history in a few words.

Without going into all the details, we need to grasp the essential principles in this seminal promise.

First, God promises there will be continual hostility between the seed of the serpent (those who are not Christians) and the seed of the woman (this refers to Christ principally and all those who follow Him). From the Bible's perspective, there is an invisible war that is far more costly than any physical war that has ever been or will be waged. It is the war for human souls and it's mainly an *ideological* war. The Bible tells us that Satan is a liar and a deceiver, the enemy of humanity who blinds people so that they will not believe the gospel (John 8:44, 2 Cor. 4:4; Rev. 12:9). He uses false ideas, philosophies, and beliefs to accomplish his sinister ends.

Second, God promises victory over Satan through the seed of the woman. For many centuries, the Jewish people looked for this person. The New Testament makes it clear that Jesus is the one promised here. He is the true seed of the woman who defeated Satan once for all at the cross, so that all those who put their faith in Him share in His victory.

Third, notice that this promise was made at the beginning of history and we have yet to see it completely fulfilled. The invisible battle rages on, to this day. In fact, the Bible makes it clear that this war will continue until Jesus returns.

We could mention the thousands of other promises God makes throughout the Bible. But this verse is enough to demonstrate the gap we referenced above. Theologians have described this gap as the 'already/not-yet' structure of history. Applying these categories to what we read in Genesis 3:15, a clear pattern emerges. Given the fall and Christ's coming in fulfillment of Genesis 3:15, the kingdom of God has 'already' begun to take root. This is why Jesus began His ministry saying, 'The time is fulfilled, and the kingdom of God is at hand; repent and believe in the gospel' (Mark 1:15).

In contrast, to the 'already' of the kingdom of God breaking into this world, we are still waiting for the 'not yet' – the ultimate triumph of the kingdom of God when Satan and sin are done away with forever. This will only happen when Jesus returns. Since the Bible does not tell us precisely when that will happen, all of us will live in the gap between the already and the not-yet.

From the biblical standpoint, the gap between these two realities explains why we suffer so much in this life. Recall our bedrock truths that sin is real and the devil is active. Since this promise was made in Genesis 3:15, Satan has been the unseen force behind much of the evil and suffering we experience, both for Christians and non-Christians.

But there is more to life in the gap between the already and the not yet than simply understanding the distance between promise and fulfillment. The New Testament tells us that history changed with the first coming of Jesus over two thousand years ago. So we need to unpack how believing the good news about what Jesus has done helps us live in the gap.

THE CENTRAL BIBLICAL PROMISE: ALL THINGS NEW

The New Testament adds nuance and hope to this general scheme of promise and fulfillment, already and not yet. With the birth of Jesus, God tells us that He has made His promises *personal*. In other words, Jesus' first coming over two thousand years ago bridged the gap. His ministry of healing, miracles, leading up to His death and resurrection were a preview of coming attractions when the gap will be closed forever. Why?

He is God's guarantee in the flesh that what He has promised *will* come to pass. This is why the apostle Paul wrote, 'For all the promises of God find their Yes in him. That is why it is through him that we utter our Amen to God for his glory' (2 Cor. 1:20). When we comprehend that Jesus fulfills all of God's promises, Paul says, we can say 'Amen,' which comes from a Hebrew word that means 'Let it be so.' Practically speaking, this means that in the midst of our life of suffering in the gap, we can say 'Let it be so,' knowing that Jesus will eventually take away all the suffering and evil in the world.

As I said, Jesus' first coming was a preview of coming attractions. Think about it like a movie, in other words. If you go to watch a film, there are a half-dozen previews before the feature movie. Some people skip these, but when I pay that much for tickets, I want to see everything, including the previews!

In the same way, Jesus' earthly ministry, recorded for us in the Gospels, tells us that the gap has been considerably shortened. He began the ultimate completion of what God had promised for millennia. What is the apex of God's promises to us? A new heaven and a new earth, a restored creation with no sin or suffering. The beautiful words of the last book in the Bible, Revelation, describe this wonderful scene. 'Then I saw a new heaven and a new earth, for the first heaven and the first earth had passed away ... He will dwell with them, and they will be his people, and God himself will be with them as their God. He will wipe away every tear from their eyes, and death shall be no more, neither shall there be mourning, nor crying, nor pain anymore, for the former things have passed away' (Rev. 21:1-4).

What a glorious vision of hope this provides! The imagery is as captivating as it is stunning – God Himself, stooping down like a caring parent to wipe away the tears from His hurting children's eyes. This is not just paradise *restored*, as Milton said. Far be it from me to correct such a literary genius, but the biblical scene we just read tells us that this is paradise *escalated*. In other words, it's not just Eden restored, but Eden made better.

How does knowing this is how the story of the universe ends help us live in the gap? Let's get at it this way. From start to finish, the Bible makes it a point to ground its claims in history. Why does the Bible make such a big deal about its historical claims?

Because, as one Jewish scholar explains, the biblical focus on history means that the Bible is not a myth. Unlike other world religions, the Bible does not evidence the hallmarks of mythological thinking precisely because it tells us that God acts *in history*. Other religions concentrate instead on the activity of the gods which are non-historical.

Therefore, as this scholar explains, the religion of Israel taught that 'the world was the domain of its one supreme God, yet within this domain there were still struggle and tension. This could no longer be interpreted mythically as a clash of divine forces. Instead, a new dimension was being called into being, the historical-moral.'[1] He goes on to explain how this view of God

---

1. Yehezkel Kaufmann, *The Religion of Israel*, trans. M. Greenberg (Chicago, IL: University of Chicago Press, 1960), p. 240; cited in John N. Oswalt, *The Bible Among the Myths* (Grand Rapids, MI: Zondervan, 2009), pp. 78-79.

and history is poles apart from any of the myths found in other religions and cultures.

The biblical claim that the creator acts within our world, in history, means that it is concerned to tell us the truth of what actually happened. This emphasis on the veracity of what it records helps us see the significance of Jesus' ministry. The New Testament places great importance on the historical facts surrounding Jesus' life – when He was born, who was ruling at the time, where He did His miracles, etc. This is why Luke's Gospel opens with these words: 'Many have undertaken to draw up an account of the things that have been fulfilled among us, just as they were handed down to us by those who from the first were eyewitnesses' (Luke 1:1-2 NIV).

In effect, Luke says, 'I am writing this account of historical facts from eyewitness testimony.' Why? He tells us a few verses later, 'so that you may know the certainty of the things you have been taught' (Luke 1:4 NIV). Like all biblical writers, Luke wants us to be certain of our faith, not simply because it is true, but because it is such an *important* truth.

If we believe that the biblical gospel is true and not just a wishful coping mechanism, everything changes. We can trust God's promises because they are *true* and have begun their ultimate fulfillment in Jesus. This knowledge will enable us to believe God is good when we are in the darkness of suffering. It will enable us to keep going when we feel like giving up.

Above all, as we have seen, the biblical worldview offers a Savior who suffers in the exact ways we have or will. When we combine this exquisite biblical portrait of Jesus' compassion for sufferers with the fact that what we read about Him is incontestably true, we have a formula for real hope when we are afflicted.

So how do we get in on this hope? The biblical answer is startling. *Simply believe*. Here's how Jesus put it. 'Truly, truly, I say to you, whoever hears my word and believes him who sent me has eternal life. He does not come into judgment, but has passed from death to life' (John 5:24).

Notice the order Jesus describes. First, we must hear His Word. We must read and listen to God's Word in the Bible. Next, we must believe what we read or hear. Did you hear the dominant note of certainty again in this promise? '*Has* eternal life.' Not 'might get eternal life,' not 'do better, try harder' and then you'll get eternal life. No. Hear, believe, receive. That's the biblical gospel in a nutshell. It really is that simple.

I think the very simplicity of the Bible's teaching on salvation is a major reason why people find it so hard to believe. 'It can't be that easy, can it?' To be clear, salvation was not easy for Jesus – we have detailed how He suffered greatly to obtain our salvation. But that's just the point. *He* suffers in *our* place so that all we have to do is believe Him and we are saved. Of course, there is more to be said. But if you are not a Christian, Jesus invites you to trust Him. Ask Him to save you and He will.

This does not mean you won't have doubts and questions – we all will, even after we embrace Jesus as our Savior. But the promise of John 5:24 *does* mean that once we believe Jesus, we are secure for eternity. We pass from death to life – real life – for the first time when we place our faith in Jesus.

Just to make sure we don't miss His point, Jesus says eternal life begins *now*. We have focused on the future aspect of it, the new heavens and new earth. But Jesus makes it clear that we also enjoy eternal life *now*. In other words, He takes the certainty of His *future* victory and offers it to us in the *present*. He has closed the gap, taking the 'not yet' and making it 'already' in our current sufferings. To repeat, knowing this with certainty is the only way to suffer with hope!

One last comment before we move on. The biblical terminology for how God saves us is 'by grace alone.' Grace simply means God's de-merited favor. That is, God shows favor to us in Jesus when we have wronged Him. That's why it's de-merited favor. We are not neutral bystanders but sinful actors on the world's stage. Despite this, God accomplishes our salvation in Jesus and offers it to us freely. All we have to do is believe.

The biblical conception of radical grace – that God does everything for our salvation and we contribute nothing – is another unique teaching of Christianity. Other religions talk a lot about grace, but there is always a caveat. You get grace *if* you do something. The 'if' in that sentence is fatal. Biblical grace in Jesus admits no 'ifs.' It is full, free, and available.

THE MOST IMPORTANT QUESTION

So, here's the most important question: Have you believed in Jesus? If not, what's holding you back? What I have written may not persuade you. You might find help in the other books in the series, all of which make a compelling case for the truth of Christianity, answering many questions skeptics have posed for centuries. Read them. Wrestle with them. Mull them over. Above all, read the Bible, bring your doubts to Jesus, and you will find Him patient, tender, and willing to meet you right where you are. All you have to do is ask Him.

Whether you have suffered much or little, you know the pain and confusion those times bring. Wouldn't it be wonderful to know that there is a trustworthy, loving God behind everything you experience? That you could talk to Him and *know* He hears you? Wouldn't that give you a new hope and purpose, even if your circumstances don't change immediately?

That's what Jesus is offering us. Right now might be a good time to put this book down and pray something like, 'Jesus, I am hurting. I don't understand your ways. But I am willing to entrust myself to you. Please meet me in my suffering and help me with my doubts. Please forgive me for my sins and make me new.' Or just pray what one man who met Jesus prayed. 'Lord, I believe; help my unbelief!' (Mark 9:24 NKJV).

From experiencing eternal life in this life, to the hope of heaven when you die, to the ultimate hope of the new heavens and new earth, the Father, Son, and Holy Spirit – the biblical God – offers us the kind of hope we all desperately want in our trials. The best part is that what God offers is not just another form of spirituality, but the *truth*. Knowing the Bible and the gospel are true makes all the difference.

CONCLUSION

Life in the gap is difficult. It can cause us to question whether or not the God of the gap is real. But Jesus has bridged the gap between promise and fulfillment. He is heaven come to earth and, having ascended back to heaven and sent the Holy Spirit to dwell in His followers, He continues to offer us a foretaste of heaven on earth.

This means that what feels like hell in this life can be transformed by faith in Jesus.

At the beginning of our study, I said our goal was not simply to survive the evil and suffering we face, but to thrive in the middle of it. The only way this will happen is if we bring our doubts, fears, questions, and unmet longings to Jesus. If you come to Him, He will say to us what He said to His first followers. 'Come to me, all who labor and are heavy laden, and I will give you rest. Take my yoke upon you, and learn from me, for I am gentle and lowly in heart' (Matt. 11:28-29).

An easy yoke for the crushing burdens of suffering in this life. A gentle and lowly Savior instead of the hard taskmasters of 'do better' philosophies and worldviews. His suffering and resurrection were for us so that we can know with certainty our suffering will end with our resurrection.

That's the gospel. It's the only answer to the question posed by this book. Will you believe it?

Suggested Further Reading

Scott Christensen, *What About Evil? A Defense of God's Sovereign Glory* (P&R Publishing, 2020).

Timothy Keller, *Walking with God Through Pain and Suffering* (Viking, 2013).

Paul David Tripp, *Suffering: Gospel Hope When Life Doesn't Make Sense* (Crossway, 2018).

Katherine Wolf and Jay Wolf, *Hope Heals: A True Story of Overwhelming Loss and Overcoming Love* (Zondervan, 2016).

Paul Wolfe, *My God is True: Lessons Learned Along Cancer's Dark Road* (Banner of Truth, 2009).

THE BIG TEN
Critical Questions Answered

SERIES EDITORS
James N. Anderson and Greg Welty

The Big Ten: Critical Questions Answered is a Christian apologetics series which addresses ten commonly asked questions about God, the Bible, and Christianity. Each book, while easy to read, is challenging and thought–provoking, dealing with subjects ranging from hell to science. A good read whatever your present opinions.

Other books available in the Big Ten series ...

*Has Science Made God
Unnecessary?*
by Ransom Poythree

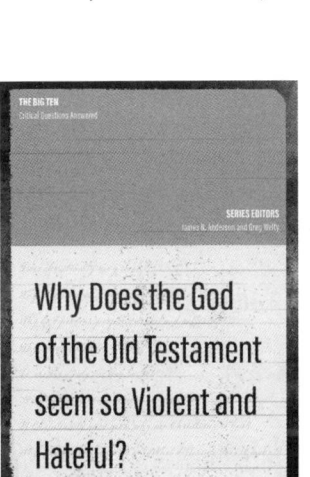

*Why Does the God of the Old
Testament seem so Violent
and Hateful?*
by Richard P. Belcher Jr.

*If Christianity is so Good,
Why are Christians so Bad?*
by Mark Coppenger

Why Should I Trust the Bible?
by Timothy Paul Jones

*How Could a Loving God
Send Anyone to Hell?*
by Benjamin M. Skaug

*Does Christianity Really
Work?*
by William Edgar

Why Is There Evil in the World (And so much of it)?

by Greg Welty

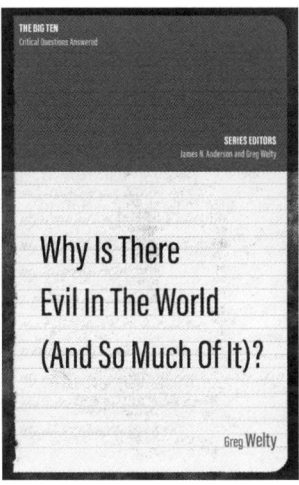

Why Should I Believe Christianity?

by James Anderson

Christian Focus Publications

Our mission statement
Staying Faithful

In dependence upon God we seek to impact the world through literature faithful to His infallible Word, the Bible. Our aim is to ensure that the Lord Jesus Christ is presented as the only hope to obtain forgiveness of sin, live a useful life and look forward to heaven with Him.

Our Books are published in four imprints:

◁◯✕ CHRISTIAN FOCUS

Popular works including biographies, commentaries, basic doctrine and Christian living.

◁◯✕ MENTOR

Books written at a level suitable for Bible College and seminary students, pastors, and other serious readers. The imprint includes commentaries, doctrinal studies, examination of current issues and church history.

◁◯✕ CHRISTIAN HERITAGE

Books representing some of the best material from the rich heritage of the church.

◁◯✕ CF4KIDS

Children's books for quality Bible teaching and for all age groups: Sunday school curriculum, puzzle and activity books; personal and family devotional titles, biographies and inspirational stories – because you are never too young to know Jesus!

Christian Focus Publications Ltd,
Geanies House, Fearn, Ross-shire,
IV20 1TW, Scotland, United Kingdom.
www.christianfocus.com